Buckle Down!®

on Massachusetts Mathematics

Book 10

ACKNOWLEDGMENT:

Massachusetts Curriculum Framework Learning Standards/MCAS Reporting Categories copyright © 1998 by Massachusetts Department of Education, which was not involved in the production of, and does not endorse, this product.

Every effort has been made by the publisher to locate each owner of the copyrighted material reprinted in this publication and to secure the necessary permissions. If there are any questions regarding the use of these materials, the publisher will take appropriate corrective measures to acknowledge ownership in future publications.

ISBN 0-7836-2054-3

Catalog #BD MA10M 1

4 5 6 7 8 9 10

President and Publisher: Douglas J. Paul, Ph.D.; Editorial Director: John Hansen; Project Editor: Gayle Palka; Editorial Assistant: Paul Meyers; Production Editor: Michael Hankes; Production Director: Jennifer Booth; Art Director: Chris Wolf; Graphic Designer: Ginny York.

TABLE OF CONTENTS

Unit 1 – Number Sense 1

Lesson 1: Mathematical Structure 2

Lesson 2: Estimation 10

Lesson 3: Discrete Mathematics 12

Test Your Skills 28

Unit 2 – Patterns, Relations, and Functions 35

Lesson 4: Algebra 36

Lesson 5: Functions 60

Lesson 6: Trigonometry 76

Test Your Skills 81

Unit 3 – Geometry and Measurement 87

Lesson 7: Geometry and Spatial Sense 88

Lesson 8: Measurement 108

Lesson 9: Geometry from an Algebraic Perspective 122

Test Your Skills 136

Unit 4 – Statistics and Probability 141

Lesson 10: Statistics 142

Lesson 11: Probability 162

Test Your Skills 169

Appendix A: General Tips for Taking Math Tests 179

Appendix B: Massachusetts Curriculum Framework: Mathematics Learning Standards, Grade 10 185

UNIT 1

Number Sense

Lesson 1: Mathematical Structure
Lesson 2: Estimation
Lesson 3: Discrete Mathematics

Lesson 1: Mathematical Structure

The Real Number System

The set of **real numbers** consists of all rational and all irrational numbers.

Rational numbers

Rational numbers include whole numbers, integers, and non-integral numbers. Any number that can be expressed in fractional form $\left(\frac{a}{b}\right)$, where a (the numerator) and b (the denominator) are both integers and the denominator is not equal to zero, is a rational number.

Whole numbers: the set of natural numbers and zero—

$\{0, 1, 2, 3, 4, 5, 6, 7, 8, \ldots\}$

Integers: the set of whole numbers and their opposites—

$I = \{\ldots\ {}^-5, {}^-4, {}^-3, {}^-2, {}^-1, 0, 1, 2, 3, 4, 5, \ldots\}$

Negative integers are less than zero. The closer they are to zero, the greater their value.

Positive integers are greater than zero. The farther away they are from zero, the greater their value.

Non-integral numbers include decimals (repeating and terminating) and fractions.

Irrational numbers

Irrational numbers cannot be expressed as the quotient of two integers in the form $\frac{a}{b}$ and they cannot be written as repeating or terminating decimals. In decimal form, the decimal representation of an irrational number goes on forever without repeating a pattern.

Practice

Directions: For Numbers 1 through 8, mark an **X** next to all **irrational** numbers. Label each **rational** number as an integer, a repeating decimal, or a terminating decimal.

1. $\sqrt{8}$ ____________

2. $\sqrt{6}$ ____________

3. $\sqrt{36}$ ____________

4. $-1.\overline{23}$ ____________

5. $\frac{23}{3}$ ____________

6. 9.80 ____________

7. −100 ____________

8. 76.98453421 . . . ____________

Number Representation and Relative Size

The **Density Property** states that between every two real numbers there is another real number. No matter how densely packed the number line is, you can always plot more numbers between two numbers.

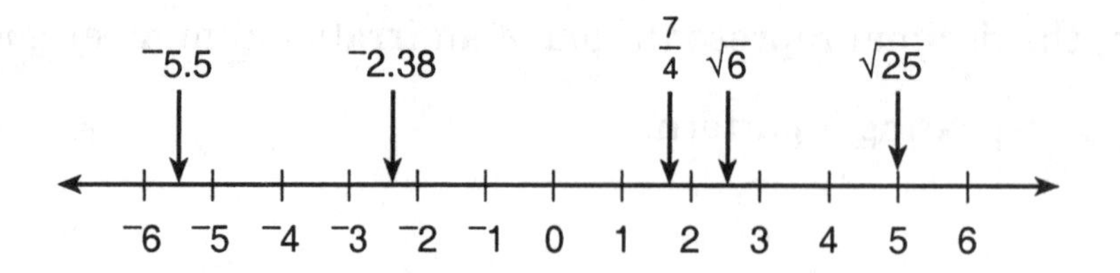

Absolute value

The **absolute value** of a real number (n) is its distance from the origin on a number line. It is shown by the symbol $|n|$.

For example, the absolute value of a non-negative number such as 50 is the number itself: $|50| = 50$. If a number is negative, drop the negative sign to find its absolute value: $|^{-}50| = 50$.

Absolute value is the **distance** a number is from zero regardless of direction.

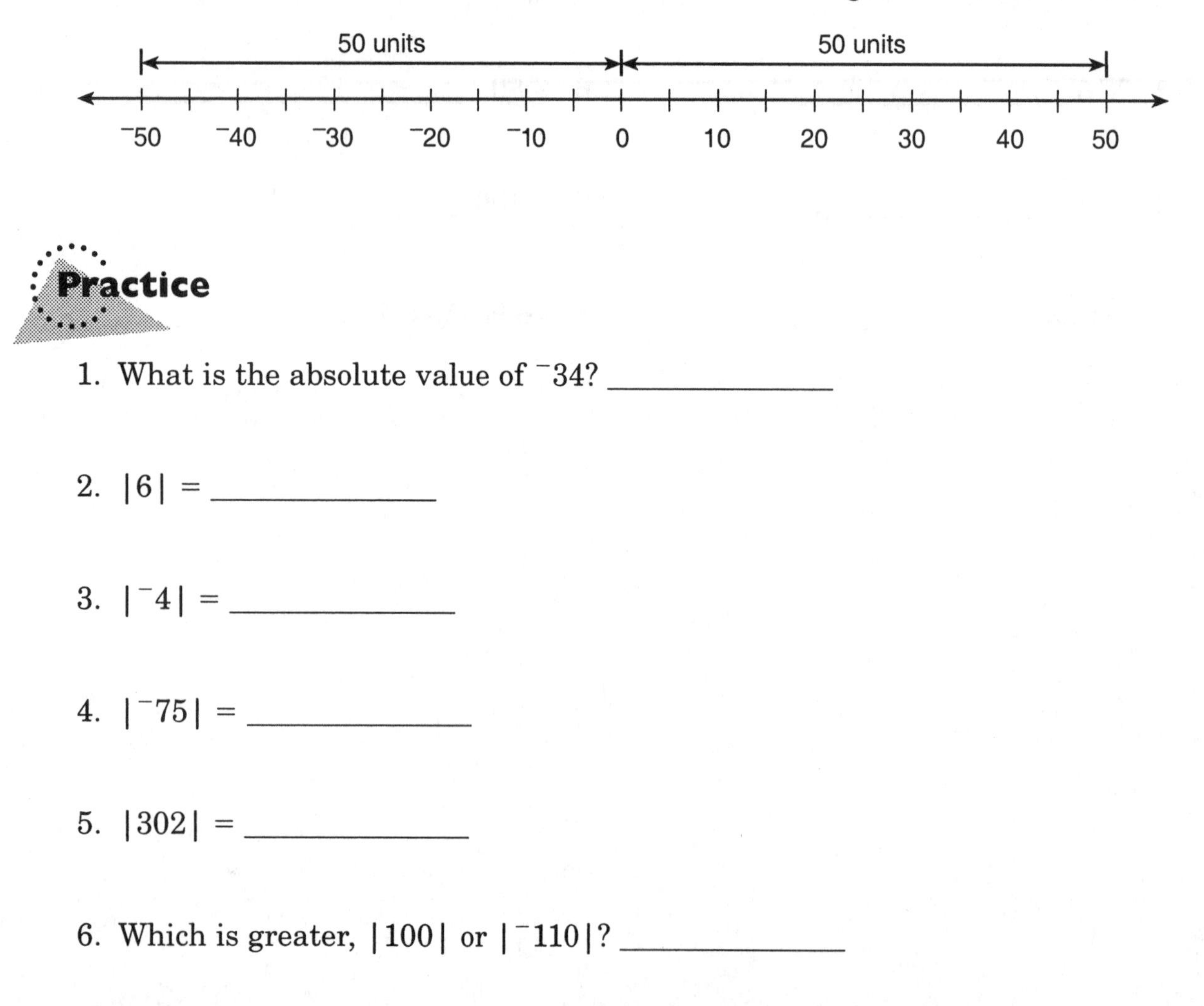

Practice

1. What is the absolute value of $^{-}34$? ______________

2. $|6| =$ ______________

3. $|^{-}4| =$ ______________

4. $|^{-}75| =$ ______________

5. $|302| =$ ______________

6. Which is greater, $|100|$ or $|^{-}110|$? ______________

Number Properties

Number properties state a relationship between numbers.

The **Commutative Property** states that the order of the numbers does not change the sum or the product:

Addition	Multiplication
$a + b = b + a$	$a \bullet b = b \bullet a$
$40 + 60 = 60 + 40$	$9 \bullet 7 = 7 \bullet 9$
$100 = 100$	$63 = 63$

The **Associative Property** states that the grouping of the numbers does not change the sum or the product.

Addition	Multiplication
$(a + b) + c = a + (b + c)$	$(a \bullet b) \bullet c = a \bullet (b \bullet c)$
$(8 + 5) + 4 = 8 + (5 + 4)$	$(6 \bullet 3) \bullet 2 = 6 \bullet (3 \bullet 2)$
$13 + 4 = 8 + 9$	$18 \bullet 2 = 6 \bullet 6$
$17 = 17$	$36 = 36$

The **Distributive Property** relates the operations of addition and multiplication.

$$a(b + c) = (a \bullet b) + (a \bullet c)$$

$$10(4 + 1) = (10 \bullet 4) + (10 \bullet 1)$$

$$10(5) = 40 + 10$$

$$50 = 50$$

Identity for Addition: The identity element for addition is 0. A number added to 0 will be equal to that same number.

$$a + 0 = a$$

$$4 + 0 = 4$$

Identity for Multiplication: The identity element for multiplication is 1. A number multiplied by 1 will be equal to that same number.

$$a \bullet 1 = a$$

$$5 \bullet 1 = 5$$

Zero Product Property: A number multiplied by zero will be equal to zero.

$$a \bullet 0 = 0$$

$$9 \bullet 0 = 0$$

Properties of equality

Reflexive Property: for each number a, $a = a$; $64 = 64$

Symmetric Property: if $a = b$ then $b = a$; if $64 = 8^2$ then $8^2 = 64$

Transitive Property: if $a = b$ and $b = c$, then $a = c$; if $64 = 8^2$ and $8^2 = 4^3$, then $64 = 4^3$

1. Use the **distributive property** to complete the following equation:

   $11(3 + 2) = (11 \bullet 3) + (\_\_\_\_\_\_\_\_\_\_)$

2. Use the **transitive property** to complete the following equation:

   if $4^2 = 16$ and $16 = 2^4$, then $4^2 =$ __________

3. Use the **associative property** to complete the following equation:

   $(20 \bullet 10) \bullet 3 = 20 \bullet (\_\_\_\_\_\_\_\_\_\_)$

Directions: Name the property or identity used in Numbers 4 through 9.

4. $1 \bullet 9 = 9$ __________

5. $7 + 53 = 53 + 7$ __________

6. $(6 + 3) \bullet 2 = 6(2) + 3(2)$ __________

7. $0 \bullet 50 = 0$ __________

8. $34 = 34$ __________

9. $1954 + 0 = 1954$ __________

Order of Operations

When working a problem that requires more than one operation, be aware of **order of operations**. Simplify all operations in expressions and equations in the following order:

1. Parentheses.
2. Exponents and square roots.
3. Multiplication and division (whichever comes first, from left to right).
4. Addition and subtraction (whichever comes first, from left to right).

Directions: Use the order of operations to solve the following problems.

1. $92 \bullet (64 \div 8) - \sqrt{144} =$ ______________

2. $8{,}240 - 652 \div 2^3 =$ ______________

Relationships Between Operations

It is also important to remember how to use **inverse operations** when solving math problems. Addition and subtraction are inverse operations; multiplication and division are inverse operations.

1. Solve for n.

   $5{,}439 + n = 439$

2. Solve for n.

   $n - 439 = 5{,}000$

3. Solve for n.

   $22n = 176$

4. Solve for n.

   $\frac{n}{50} = 625$

Relationships Between Algebraic Procedures and Geometric Concepts

Some algebraic procedures become more apparent when you apply geometric ideas and concepts to actually create a geometric model for the problem.

Example

Look at a geometric model of areas made with algebra tiles and arranged in a rectangular array to help explain the algebraic procedure of squaring a binomial. $(x + y)^2 = x^2 + 2xy + y^2$.

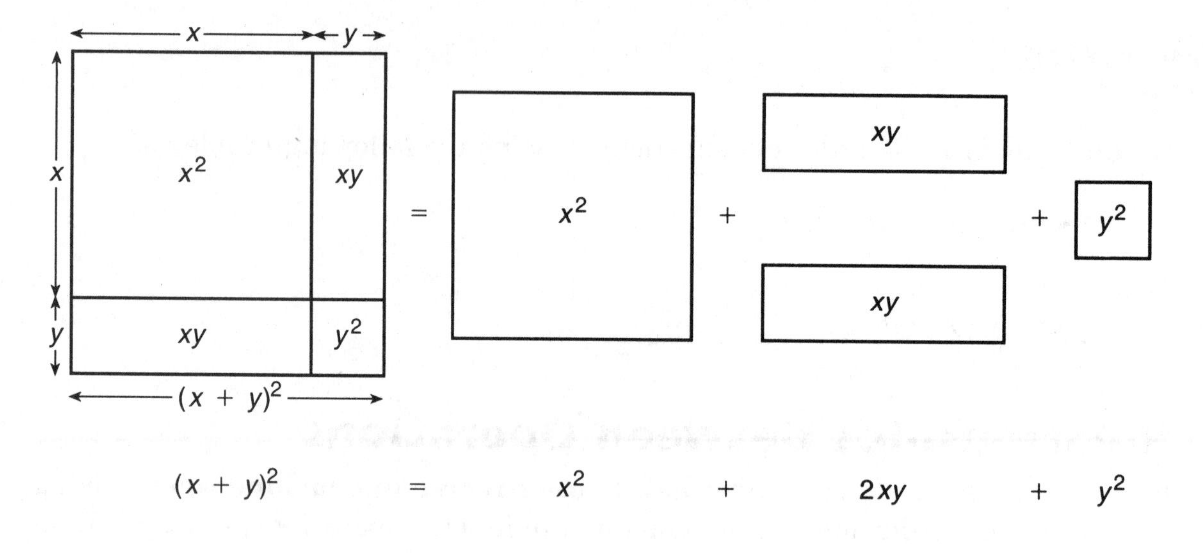

Example

This geometric model of algebra tiles shows the product of $(x + 1)(x + 3) = x^2 + 4x + 3$.

x
3
(x + 1)
x²
x x x x
x 3
1
(x + 3)
= x² + x x x x + 3

$(x + 1)(x + 3) = x^2 + 4x + 3$

Creating geometric models from algebra tiles for the product of two polynomials helps you see some of the factoring patterns for quadratic trinomials and other polynomials. It also helps you decide if a polynomial can be factored. If you can't arrange the tiles in a rectangular array, the polynomial can't be factored.

Practice

Directions: Use the geometric models in Numbers 1 through 3 to help you factor the quadratic expressions.

1. $x^2 + 5x + 4 = (x + \_\_\_\_\_)(x + \_\_\_\_\_)$

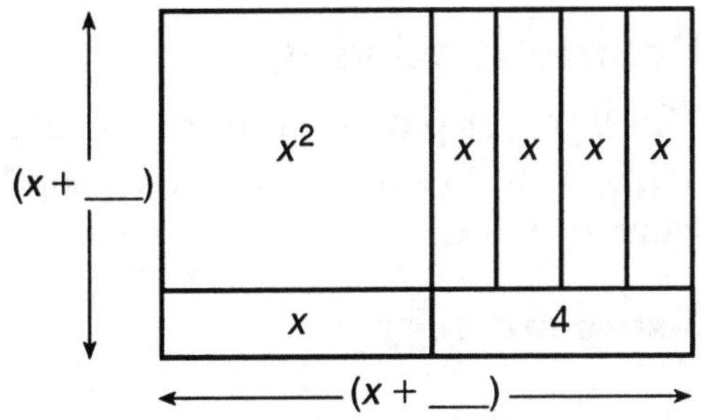

$(x + \_\_)$ | x^2 | x | x | x | x | x | 4 | $(x + \_\_)$

$x^2 + 5x + 4 = (x + \_\_)(x + \_\_)$

2. $x^2 + 6x + 8 = (x + \_\_\_\_\_)(x + \_\_\_\_\_)$

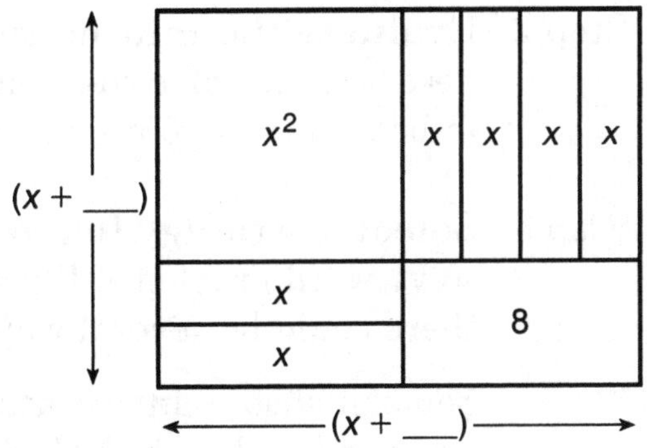

$(x + \_\_)$ | x^2 | x | x | x | x | x | x | 8 | $(x + \_\_)$

$x^2 + 6x + 8 = (x + \_\_)(x + \_\_)$

3. $x^2 + 7x + 12 = (x + \_\_\_\_\_)(x + \_\_\_\_\_)$

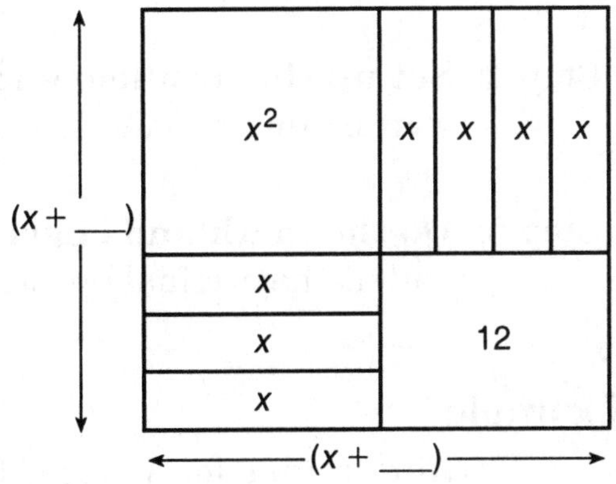

$(x + \_\_)$ | x^2 | x | x | x | x | x | x | x | 12 | $(x + \_\_)$

$x^2 + 7x + 12 = (x + \_\_)(x + \_\_)$

Lesson 2: Estimation

Before you calculate math answers, it's a good idea to first **estimate** a solution to the problem. Having some idea of what your answer should be will alert you to careless errors and help you to check the reasonableness of your answer.

Problem solving

The hardest part of a math word problem is trying to understand what you're being asked to do. Below is a step-by-step strategy to help you simplify math word problems.

5-step strategy

Step 1: **Take time to study the problem.** Think carefully about what you are actually being asked to do. Sometimes a problem may sound complicated when it is actually quite simple.

Step 2: **Evaluate the information given.** Focus on the information necessary to solve the problem. Sometimes it helps to write the information in your own words.

Step 3: **Select a strategy for solving the problem.** There are many ways to solve word problems. If you gave the same problem to 10 students, there could be several ways of solving it, but only one correct answer.

You can choose an operation or operations, write an equation, make a table or list, break the original problem into simpler problems, visualize or draw a picture (such as a Venn diagram, graph, pattern, etc., —anything that will help you "see" the math), work backwards, or guess and check.

Step 4: **Set up the problem and estimate a reasonable answer.** Does your estimate make sense based on the information given?

Step 5: **Do the math and check your final answer.** Look at your estimate and at the original question. Did you answer what you were asked?

After saving for 3 years, Troy bought a used car for $3,895. He had $5,000 in his savings account before he withdrew the money for his car. What percent of his savings did Troy spend on his car?

Troy's used car = $3,895

Troy's savings account before the purchase = $5,000

Does it matter how long Troy has saved his money? No.

You can mentally round \$3,895 to \$4,000—a reasonable estimate is $\frac{4}{5}$ or 80%. This is an important step that will help you catch careless errors. For example, if you divided 4,000 by 5,000 (or $\frac{4}{5}$) and estimated that Troy spent 125% of his savings on the car, would this make sense?

No.

Now do the math and check your final answer.

$$\frac{\$3{,}895}{\$5{,}000} = 0.779$$

Convert to a percent: 0.779 = 77.9%.

1. Maurice is the 10th-grade reporter for the school newspaper. He claims that 0.1% of the population of the state of Massachusetts attended a rock concert at the local civic center. The 1990 population of Massachusetts was 6,016,425. Use this information to estimate the number of people who may have attended the concert. Explain how you arrived at your estimate and justify it mathematically.

___

___

___

2. Sarah sold 39 submarine sandwiches Monday. Assuming business remains about the same, estimate how many submarine sandwiches Sarah should expect to sell Tuesday through Friday.

___

3. The population for Massachusetts in 1980 was 5,737,037. The population increased and was 6,016,425 in 1990. Estimate the percent of increase in population from 1980 to 1990. Explain how you arrived at your estimate and justify it mathematically.

___

___

___

Lesson 3: Discrete Mathematics

Discrete mathematics is a topic in math where more than one correct solution may exist for a problem. Your task is to find the best solution for the given situation.

Matrices

A **matrix** is a rectangular array of numbers. These numbers (called entries or elements) are written between parentheses or brackets.

$$\begin{pmatrix} 2 & 3 \\ 4 & 5 \\ 6 & 7 \end{pmatrix} \quad \begin{bmatrix} 9 & 2 & 4 \\ 3 & 5 & 7 \end{bmatrix}$$

The **dimensions** of a matrix are determined by the number of rows and columns.

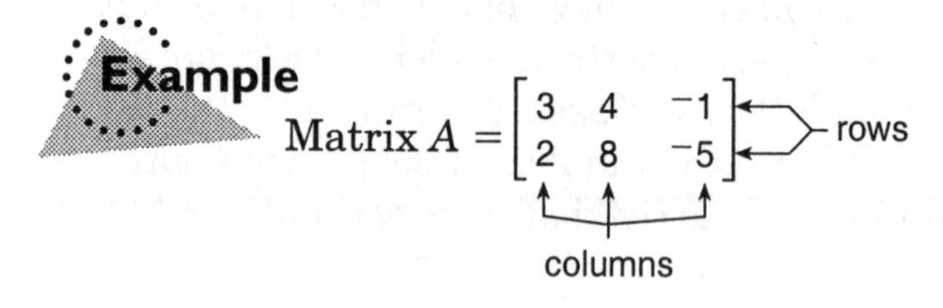

The matrix above has two rows and three columns. Therefore, it is a 2×3 matrix. This is called the **order** of the matrix.

Directions: Write the order of each matrix for Numbers 1 and 2.

1. $\begin{bmatrix} 2 & 6 \\ 8 & 3 \end{bmatrix}$

2. $\begin{bmatrix} 9 & 1 & 0 & -5 \\ 7 & -3 & 2 & 6 \end{bmatrix}$

3. Construct a 3×3 matrix.

Matrix addition

Two matrices can be **added** together only if they have the **same dimensions**.

Example

$A = \begin{bmatrix} 1 & 3 & 8 \\ 5 & 2 & 4 \end{bmatrix} \qquad B = \begin{bmatrix} ^-1 & 4 & ^-2 \\ 6 & 10 & 7 \end{bmatrix} \qquad C = \begin{bmatrix} ^-1 & 6 \\ 4 & 10 \\ ^-2 & 7 \end{bmatrix}$

Matrices A and B can be added together because they are both 2×3 matrices. The result will be a 2×3 matrix.

However, matrix C cannot be added to A or B because it is not a 2×3 matrix. Matrix C is a 3×2 matrix.

Matrices are added by adding the elements in one matrix to the corresponding elements in the other matrix.

Find $A + B$.

$A = \begin{bmatrix} 1 & 3 & 8 \\ 5 & 2 & 4 \end{bmatrix} \qquad B = \begin{bmatrix} ^-1 & 4 & ^-2 \\ 6 & 10 & 7 \end{bmatrix}$

$$\begin{bmatrix} 1 + {^-1} & 3 + 4 & 8 + {^-2} \\ 5 + 6 & 2 + 10 & 4 + 7 \end{bmatrix} = \begin{bmatrix} 0 & 7 & 6 \\ 11 & 12 & 11 \end{bmatrix}$$

A B A B A B

The result is a 2×3 matrix.

Elements of a matrix also are identified by their position in rows and columns.

For example, 0 is in row 1, column 1, so its position is 1, 1.

The element in position 2, 3 is 11.

Matrix multiplication

To multiply two matrices the number of columns in the first matrix must equal the number of rows in the second matrix.

Example

$$A = \begin{bmatrix} 2 & 5 \\ 3 & 1 \end{bmatrix} \qquad B = \begin{bmatrix} 4 & 8 \\ 7 & 6 \end{bmatrix}$$

Step 1: **Find the element in position 1, 1.**

$$\begin{bmatrix} 2 & 5 \\ & \end{bmatrix}\begin{bmatrix} 4 & \\ 7 & \end{bmatrix} = \begin{bmatrix} (2 \bullet 4) + (5 \bullet 7) \\ 8 + 35 \end{bmatrix} = \begin{bmatrix} \textcircled{43} & \\ & \end{bmatrix}$$

Step 2: **Find the element in position 2, 1.**

$$\begin{bmatrix} & \\ 3 & 1 \end{bmatrix}\begin{bmatrix} 4 & \\ 7 & \end{bmatrix} = \begin{bmatrix} (3 \bullet 4) + (1 \bullet 7) \\ 12 + 7 \end{bmatrix} = \begin{bmatrix} 43 & \\ \textcircled{19} & \end{bmatrix}$$

Step 3: **Find the element in position 1, 2.**

$$\begin{bmatrix} 2 & 5 \\ & \end{bmatrix}\begin{bmatrix} & 8 \\ & 6 \end{bmatrix} = \begin{bmatrix} (2 \bullet 8) + (5 \bullet 6) \\ 16 + 30 \end{bmatrix} = \begin{bmatrix} 43 & \textcircled{46} \\ 19 & \end{bmatrix}$$

Step 4: **Find the element in position 2, 2.**

$$\begin{bmatrix} & \\ 3 & 1 \end{bmatrix}\begin{bmatrix} & 8 \\ & 6 \end{bmatrix} = \begin{bmatrix} (3 \bullet 8) + (1 \bullet 6) \\ 24 + 6 \end{bmatrix} = \begin{bmatrix} 43 & 46 \\ 19 & \textcircled{30} \end{bmatrix}$$

$$\begin{bmatrix} 2 & 5 \\ 3 & 1 \end{bmatrix}\begin{bmatrix} 4 & 8 \\ 7 & 6 \end{bmatrix} = \begin{bmatrix} 43 & 46 \\ 19 & 30 \end{bmatrix}$$

Matrix properties

Matrices are another finite system where real number properties apply.

Example

This is the 2×2 identity matrix for addition. $\begin{bmatrix} 0 & 0 \\ 0 & 0 \end{bmatrix}$

A matrix added to the identity matrix will be equal to that same matrix.

$$\begin{bmatrix} a & b \\ c & d \end{bmatrix} + \begin{bmatrix} 0 & 0 \\ 0 & 0 \end{bmatrix} = \begin{bmatrix} a & b \\ c & d \end{bmatrix}$$

$$\begin{bmatrix} 5 & -3 \\ 1 & 28 \end{bmatrix} + \begin{bmatrix} 0 & 0 \\ 0 & 0 \end{bmatrix} = \begin{bmatrix} 5 & -3 \\ 1 & 28 \end{bmatrix}$$

Example

This is the 2×2 identity matrix for multiplication. $\begin{bmatrix} 1 & 0 \\ 0 & 1 \end{bmatrix}$

A matrix multiplied by the identity matrix will be equal to that same matrix.

$$\begin{bmatrix} 3 & 4 \\ 5 & 6 \end{bmatrix} \begin{bmatrix} 1 & 0 \\ 0 & 1 \end{bmatrix} = \begin{bmatrix} 3 & 4 \\ 5 & 6 \end{bmatrix}$$

Practice

Directions: Use the following matrices to answer Numbers 1 through 6.

$$P = \begin{bmatrix} 2 & 4 \\ 3 & 8 \end{bmatrix} \qquad Q = \begin{bmatrix} 1 & 6 \\ 4 & 2 \end{bmatrix} \qquad R = \begin{bmatrix} 0 & 0 \\ 0 & 0 \end{bmatrix} \qquad S = \begin{bmatrix} 1 & 0 \\ 0 & 1 \end{bmatrix}$$

1. Find $P + Q$. ____________
2. Find PQ. ____________
3. Find $P + R$. ____________
4. Find QS. ____________
5. Find PR. ____________
6. Find RS. ____________

Application of matrices

Example

A contractor is building an apartment complex featuring one-, two-, and three-bedroom units. Each unit comes in two different floor plans. The matrix P (for production) tells the number of each type of unit for this development.

$$P = \begin{array}{c} \text{Plan 1} \quad \text{Plan 2} \\ \begin{bmatrix} 10 & 5 \\ 25 & 10 \\ 15 & 10 \end{bmatrix} \end{array} \begin{array}{l} \\ \text{1 bedroom} \\ \text{2 bedroom} \\ \text{3 bedroom} \end{array}$$

The matrix M (for materials) gives the amounts of lumber, concrete, fixtures, and labor needed for each floor plan.

$$M = \begin{array}{c} \text{Lumber} \quad \text{Concrete} \quad \text{Fixtures} \quad \text{Labor} \\ \begin{bmatrix} 6 & 7 & 9 & 18 \\ 7 & 8 & 9 & 20 \end{bmatrix} \end{array} \begin{array}{l} \\ \text{Plan 1} \\ \text{Plan 2} \end{array}$$

The matrix product PM gives the total amount of material needed for the development.

$$PM = \begin{array}{c} \text{Plan 1} \quad \text{Plan 2} \\ \begin{bmatrix} 10 & 5 \\ 25 & 10 \\ 15 & 10 \end{bmatrix} \end{array} \begin{array}{c} \text{Lumber} \quad \text{Concrete} \quad \text{Fixtures} \quad \text{Labor} \\ \begin{bmatrix} 6 & 7 & 9 & 18 \\ 7 & 8 & 9 & 20 \end{bmatrix} \end{array}$$

$$= \begin{array}{c} \text{Lumber} \quad \text{Concrete} \quad \text{Fixtures} \quad \text{Labor} \\ \begin{bmatrix} 60 + 35 & 70 + 40 & 90 + 45 & 180 + 100 \\ 150 + 70 & 175 + 80 & 225 + 90 & 450 + 200 \\ 90 + 70 & 105 + 80 & 135 + 90 & 270 + 200 \end{bmatrix} \end{array} \begin{array}{l} \\ \text{1 bedroom} \\ \text{2 bedroom} \\ \text{3 bedroom} \end{array}$$

$$= \begin{array}{c} \text{Lumber} \quad \text{Concrete} \quad \text{Fixtures} \quad \text{Labor} \\ \begin{bmatrix} 95 & 110 & 135 & 280 \\ 220 & 255 & 315 & 650 \\ 160 & 185 & 225 & 470 \end{bmatrix} \end{array} \begin{array}{l} \\ \text{1 bedroom} \\ \text{2 bedroom} \\ \text{3 bedroom} \end{array}$$

Practice

Directions: The cost of each unit of material is given by the matrix C (for cost).

Cost per unit

$$C = \begin{bmatrix} 700 \\ 80 \\ 900 \\ 1{,}000 \end{bmatrix} \begin{matrix} \text{Lumber} \\ \text{Concrete} \\ \text{Fixtures} \\ \text{Labor} \end{matrix}$$

Use this information and the previous example to answer Numbers 1 and 2.

1. Determine the total cost of each model for this development by multiplying matrix PM by matrix C. Express in matrix form.

2. Find the average cost for each unit.

Sequences

A **sequence** is a set of numbers (called terms) arranged in a certain order. Sequences are either finite or infinite.

In a **finite** sequence, it is possible to count the number of terms in the sequence.

1, 4, 7, 10, 13 is a finite sequence that includes five terms.

An **infinite** sequence contains an infinite number of terms.

1, 4, 7, 10, 13, . . . is an infinite sequence. We can't count the number of terms.

Ellipses (. . .) indicate that the numbers follow the pattern into infinity.

Arithmetic sequences

An **arithmetic sequence** of numbers is a sequence where the **difference** between any two consecutive terms is constant. This is called the **common difference (*d*)**.

Examples

2, 5, 8, 11, 14 — This is an arithmetic sequence whose common difference is 3.

32, 26, 20, 14, 8, . . . — This is an arithmetic sequence whose common difference is -6.

1, 2, 4, 7, 11, . . . — This is **not** an arithmetic sequence because the difference between consecutive numbers is not constant.

Geometric sequences

A **geometric sequence** of numbers is a sequence where the **ratio** of any two consecutive terms is constant. This ratio is called the **common ratio (*r*)**.

Examples

2, 6, 18, 54 — This is a geometric sequence whose common ratio is 3.

1000, 200, 40, 8, . . . — This is a geometric sequence whose common ratio is 0.2 or $\frac{1}{5}$.

5, 10, 15, 20, . . . — This is **not** a geometric sequence because a common ratio does not exist between any two consecutive terms.

Fibonacci sequence

Leonardo Fibonacci was an Italian mathematician who discovered an interesting pattern that shows up in nature.

0, 1, 1, 2, 3, 5, 8, 13, 21, 34, 55, 89, 144, . . .

Each term in the series is the sum of the two terms before it.

What would be the next two terms in this Fibonacci sequence? ______________

1. Look at this **arithmetic** sequence.

   9, 12, 15, ______ , 21, ______

   A. What is the common difference of this sequence? ______________

   B. Find the missing terms. ______________

2. Look at this **geometric** sequence.

   15, 30, 60, ______ , 240

   A. What is the common ratio of this sequence? ______________

   B. Find the missing term. ______________

Directions: For Numbers 3 through 6, tell whether the sequence is arithmetic, geometric, Fibonacci-like, or none of these.

3. 1, 4, 9, 16, 25, 36, . . . ______________

4. 7, 11, 15, 19, . . . ______________

5. 3, 4, 7, 11, 18, 29, . . . ______________

6. 512, 128, 32, 8, 2, . . . ______________

The nth Term

Notation such as $a_1, a_2, a_3, \ldots, a_n$ is used to represent the terms of a sequence. The **subscripts** identify the position of the terms in the sequence.

term in the sequence → a_1

↑

subscript

a_1 represents the **1st** term in the sequence

a_2 represents the **2nd** term in the sequence

a_3 represents the **3rd** term in the sequence

The ***n*th** term of a sequence is denoted by a_n where n represents the position of the term in a sequence. The ***n*th** term can be any term.

Example

This is an arithmetic sequence where $d = 3$.

3,	6,	9,	12,	15,	. . . ,
↓	↓	↓	↓	↓	↓
a_1	a_2	a_3	a_4	a_5	a_n

To get terms in this sequence, multiply the subscript by 3; the nth term is $a_n = 3n$

What would be the 10th term in the sequence?

Since $a_n = 3n$,

$a_{10} = 3 \bullet 10 = 30$

Explicit and Recursive Definitions of a Sequence

Explicit and **recursive** definitions are formulas that can be used to find terms without having to extend the sequence.

Explicit definition

This definition allows us to calculate any term in the sequence in a very direct way. No preceding terms are needed to calculate any of the other terms.

Use this formula to find any term in an arithmetic sequence:

$$a_n = a_1 + (n - 1)d$$

a_1 is the first term, n is the position of the term, and d is the common difference.

Example

This is an arithmetic sequence whose common difference is 4.

1, 5, 9, 13, 17, . . .

Using the formula, you can justify the terms of the sequence.

$$\boldsymbol{a_n = a_1 + (n - 1) \bullet 4}$$

$\boldsymbol{a_1} = 1 + (1 - 1) \bullet 4 = 1 + (0) \bullet 4 = 1 + 0 = \mathbf{1}$ (1st term)

$\boldsymbol{a_2} = 1 + (2 - 1) \bullet 4 = 1 + (1) \bullet 4 = 1 + 4 = \mathbf{5}$ (2nd term)

$\boldsymbol{a_3} = 1 + (3 - 1) \bullet 4 = 1 + (2) \bullet 4 = 1 + 8 = \mathbf{9}$ (3rd term)

$\boldsymbol{a_4} = 1 + (4 - 1) \bullet 4 = 1 + (3) \bullet 4 = 1 + 12 = \mathbf{13}$ (4th term)

$\boldsymbol{a_5} = 1 + (5 - 1) \bullet 4 = 1 + (4) \bullet 4 = 1 + 16 = \mathbf{17}$ (5th term)

What would be the 100th term in the sequence? ______________

Example

The Wall of Photos opens for business on January 1 with 500 posters to give away as a promotion. Each day, 4 posters are given away. How many posters are left when the store opens on the day of January 14?

Day of promotion	1	2	3	4
Posters remaining	500	496	492	488

Use the explicit definition of an arithmetic sequence to find the 14th term. (This will represent the number of posters remaining at the opening on the 14th day of the promotion.)

$\boldsymbol{a_n = a_1 + (n - 1)d}$ $\boldsymbol{a_1} = 500$ and $\boldsymbol{d} = 4$

$$a_{14} = 500 + (14 - 1) \bullet ({}^{-}4)$$
$$= 500 + 13 \bullet ({}^{-}4)$$
$$= 500 - 52$$
$$= 448 \text{ posters}$$

You also can find any term in a **geometric sequence** if you know the first term and the common ratio.

Use this formula to find any term in a geometric sequence:

$$a_n = a_1 r^{(n - 1)}$$

a_1 is the first term, n is the position of the term, and r is the common ratio.

Example

This is a geometric sequence whose common ratio is 5.

4, 20, 100, 500, . . .

Using the formula, you can justify the terms of this sequence.

$$a_n = a_1 r^{(n - 1)}$$

$a_1 = 4 \bullet 5^{(1 - 1)} = 4 \bullet 5^0 = 4 \bullet 1 = 4$ (1st term)

$a_2 = 4 \bullet 5^{(2 - 1)} = 4 \bullet 5^1 = 4 \bullet 5 = 20$ (2nd term)

$a_3 = 4 \bullet 5^{(3 - 1)} = 4 \bullet 5^2 = 4 \bullet 25 = 100$ (3rd term)

$a_4 = 4 \bullet 5^{(4 - 1)} = 4 \bullet 5^3 = 4 \bullet 125 = 500$ (4th term)

What would be the 50th term in the sequence? _______________

What would be the 100th term in the sequence? _______________

Example

Antoinette's grandparents put $250 into a college fund on the day she was born. If this fund earns 8% interest annually, how much will it be worth when all of the money in the account is given to Antoinette on her 18th birthday?

Birthday	1	2	3
Amount in fund	250 + 250 • 0.08 = 270	270 + 270 • 0.08 = 291.60	291.60 + 291.60 • 0.08 = 314.93

Use the explicit definition of a geometric sequence to find the 18th term. (This will represent the amount in the fund on Antoinette's 18th birthday.)

$a_n = a_1 r^{(n-1)}$ $\qquad a_1 = 270$ and $r = 1.08 \left(\frac{270}{250}\right)$

$a_{18} = 270 \bullet 1.08^{17}$ ← (1.08 to the 17th power ≈ 3.7)

$= 270 \bullet 3.7$

$= \$999.00$

Practice

Directions: Use the sequence below to answer Numbers 1 through 3.

6, 9, 12, 15, . . .

1. Is this an arithmetic or a geometric sequence? ____________________

2. Which formula should you use to find the *n*th term? ____________________

3. What is the 25th term in the sequence? ____________________

Recursive definitions

A **recursive** definition describes a sequence whose terms are defined by means of one or more preceding terms. Known terms are used to calculate new terms, new terms become known terms and are used to calculate further new terms, and so on.

The **recursive** definition for an **arithmetic sequence** is as follows:

$$\begin{cases} \boldsymbol{a_1} \\ \boldsymbol{a_n = (a_{n-1}) + d, \textit{for } n > 1} \end{cases}$$

a_1 = the first term

a_{n-1} = the term immediately preceding a_n

d = the common difference

Example

Use the formula to justify the terms of the following sequence:

5, 9, 13, 17, . . .

$$\begin{cases} a_1 = 5 \\ a_n = (a_{n-1}) + 4, \text{ for } n > 1 \end{cases}$$

$\boldsymbol{a_1} = 5$ (1st term)

$\boldsymbol{a_2} = (a_{2-1}) + 4 = a_1 + 4 = 5 + 4 = \mathbf{9}$ (2nd term)

$\boldsymbol{a_3} = (a_{3-1}) + 4 = a_2 + 4 = 9 + 4 = \mathbf{13}$ (3rd term)

$\boldsymbol{a_4} = (a_{4-1}) + 4 = a_3 + 4 = 13 + 4 = \mathbf{17}$ (4th term)

Practice

1. What would be the 5th term in the sequence above? ____________________

2. What would be the 7th term in the sequence above? ____________________

The **recursive** definition of a geometric sequence is as follows:

$$\begin{cases} \boldsymbol{a_1} \\ \boldsymbol{a_n = (a_{n-1}) \bullet r, \textit{ for } n > 1} \end{cases}$$

a_1 = the first term

a_{n-1} = the term immediately preceding a_n

r = the common ratio

Example

Use the formula to justify the terms of the following sequence:

4, 20, 100, 500, . . .

$$\begin{cases} a_1 = 4 \\ a_n = (a_{n-1}) \bullet 5, \text{ for } n > 1 \end{cases}$$

$\boldsymbol{a_1} = 4$ (1st term)

$\boldsymbol{a_2} = (a_{2-1}) \bullet 5 = a_1 \bullet 5 = 4 \bullet 5 = \mathbf{20}$ (2nd term)

$\boldsymbol{a_3} = (a_{3-1}) \bullet 5 = a_2 \bullet 5 = 20 \bullet 5 = \mathbf{100}$ (3rd term)

$\boldsymbol{a_4} = (a_{4-1}) \bullet 5 = a_3 \bullet 5 = 100 \bullet 5 = \mathbf{500}$ (4th term)

Practice

1. What would be the 5th term in the sequence above? ____________________

2. What would be the 7th term in the sequence above? ____________________

Special Investigation: Networks and Paths

Finding solutions to routing problems usually involves analyzing finite graphs. When values are assigned to the edges, the graph is called a **weighted finite graph**.

Example

A salesman must call on customers in West Springfield. Each edge of the graph shows the actual mileage between two cities. What is the best traceable path (the one with the fewest total miles) if he is based in Amherst?

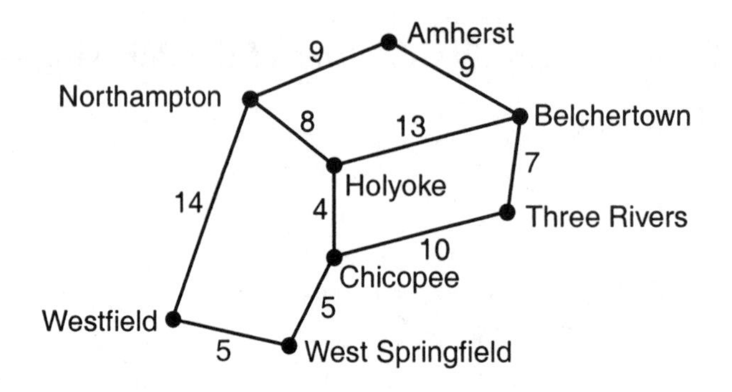

There are several traceable paths from Amherst to West Springfield. Keep in mind you are looking for the smallest edges, and the most direct route is not necessarily the best traceable path.

Solution 1:

Amherst→Northampton→Westfield→West Springfield (28)

Solution 2:

Amherst→Northampton→Holyoke→Chicopee→West Springfield (26)

Solution 3:

Amherst→Belchertown→Holyoke→Chicopee→West Springfield (31)

Solution 4:

Amherst→Belchertown→Three Rivers→Chicopee→West Springfield (31)

The best traceable path, based on actual total miles, is Amherst→Northampton→Holyoke→Chickopee→West Springfield

Venn Diagrams

To represent data, it is useful to visualize the problem by drawing a Venn diagram.

1. At Washington High School, a total of 28 students play soccer, basketball, and/or volleyball. Of these students, 20 play soccer, 10 play basketball, and 15 play volleyball; 7 students play both soccer and basketball, 9 play both soccer and volleyball, 5 play both basketball and volleyball, and 4 students play all three sports. How many of the students play only soccer, basketball, or volleyball? Draw a Venn diagram and solve the problem.

2. Fill in the rest of the Venn diagram below to show the relationship between Set A = {5, 10, 15} and Set B = {10, 20, 30}.

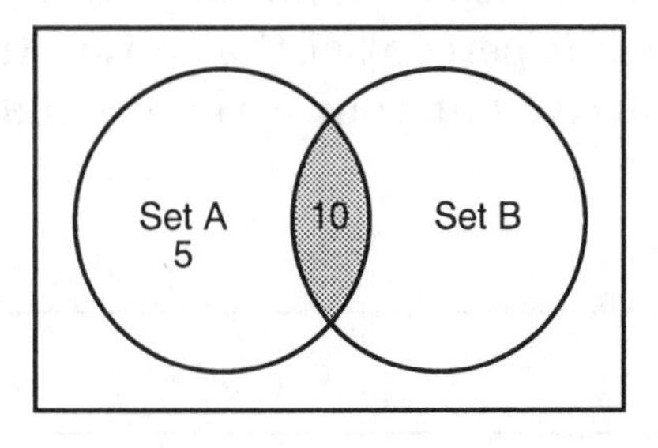

3. In the space below, draw a Venn diagram to show the relationship between Set B and Set C.

   Set B = {10, 20, 30} Set C = {5, 10, 15, 20, 30}

Test Your Skills

1. Which expression below is greatest?

   A. $0.9 \bullet 52$

   B. $\sqrt{625}$

   C. 33

   D. $\frac{1}{4}$ of 110

2. Which of the following is an **irrational** number?

   A. $74.\overline{54}$

   B. $\frac{22}{7}$

   C. 12

   D. $3\frac{1}{3}$

3. Jordan received a $2,000 college scholarship. His college tuition is $10,356.88. Estimate what percent of the tuition the scholarship money will pay. Explain how you arrived at your estimate and justify it mathematically.

   ____

   ____

   ____

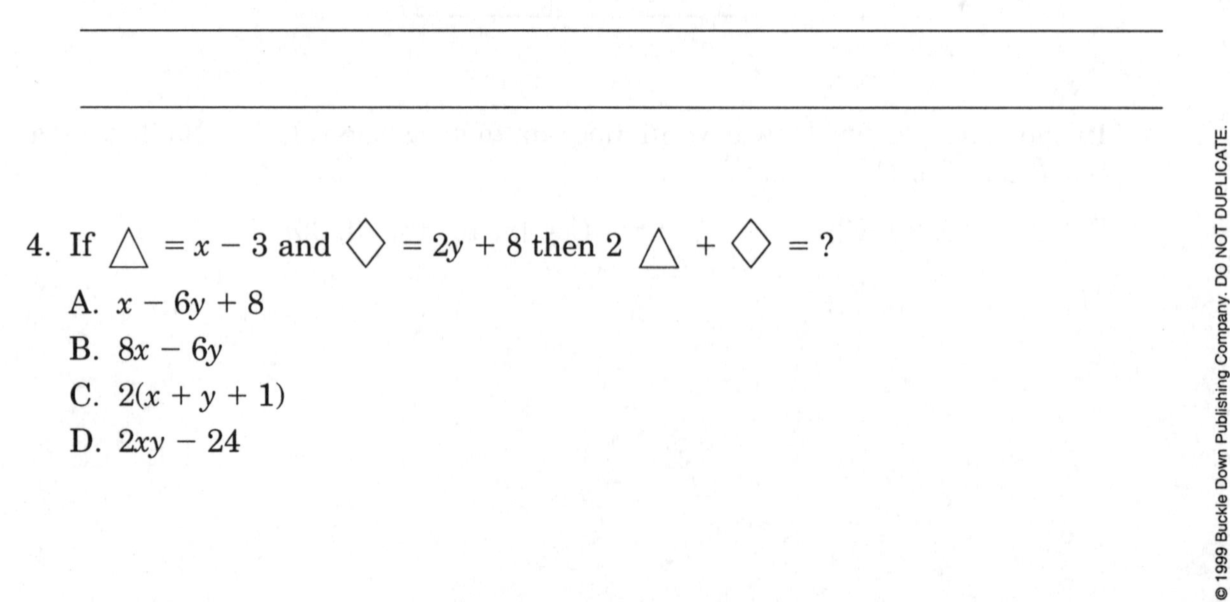

4. If △ $= x - 3$ and ◇ $= 2y + 8$ then 2 △ + ◇ = ?

   A. $x - 6y + 8$

   B. $8x - 6y$

   C. $2(x + y + 1)$

   D. $2xy - 24$

5. What would be the 25th term in this sequence? ____________

   3, 7, 11, 15, 19, 23, . . .

6. Which expression represents the number of dots in a triangle with n dots on the bottom?

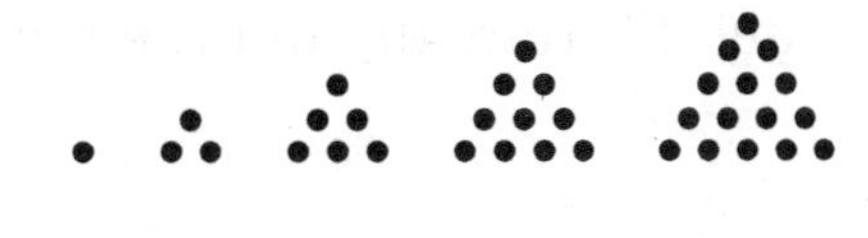

   A. $2n + n$
   B. $0.5n(n + 1)$
   C. $2n - 1$
   D. $2n + 1$

7. What is the value of x when n is 38? ____________

x	23	19	15	11	
n	14	20	26	32	38

8. Which of the strategies below will best help you solve the following problem?

   Paul, Ringo, John, and George are waiting in line. Paul is in front of John. John is between George and Ringo. Ringo is last. Who is second in line?

   A. drawing a picture
   B. choosing an operation
   C. writing an equation
   D. finding a pattern

9. Solve.

   $5^2 + (7 - 5) - 2 \bullet 4 \div 2 = ?$

   A. 10
   B. 23
   C. 50
   D. 54

10. Lena has to correctly answer 32 out of 40 questions to qualify for the state finals in history. What could she do to estimate the percent of questions she needs to answer correctly?

    A. round 32 to 30, add 30 to 40, and then divide the sum by 2
    B. round 32 to 30, divide 30 by 40, and then multiply the quotient by 100
    C. round 32 to 30, multiply 30 by 40, and then divide the product by 100
    D. round 32 to 30, subtract 30 from 40, and then multiply the difference by 100

11. 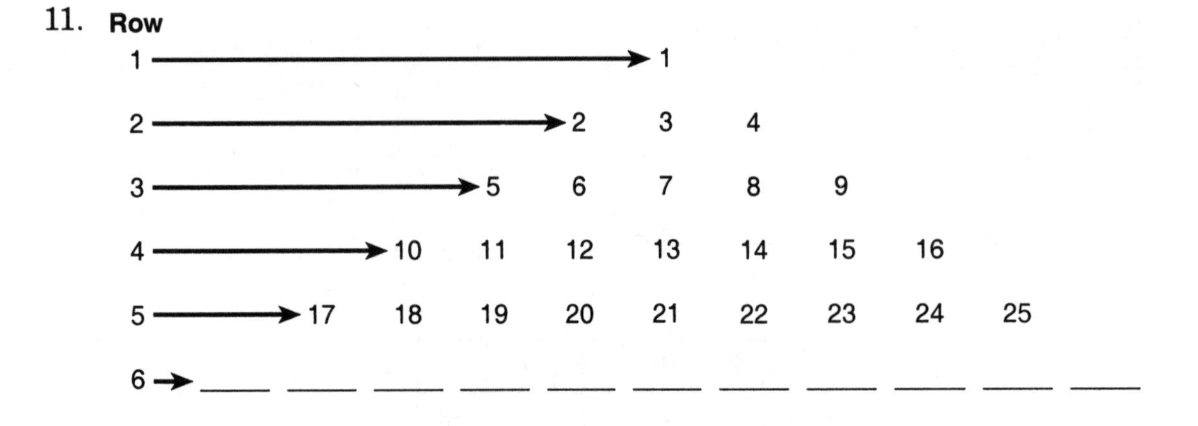

    A. Complete row 6.

    B. There are different ways of describing this pattern. Briefly explain how you would determine which numbers would be in the 9th row.

12. Express the number 256 in two other ways.

____

____

Directions: Use the following matrices to answer Number 13.

$Q = \begin{bmatrix} 4 & 7 \\ 1 & 3 \end{bmatrix}$ $Y = \begin{bmatrix} 2 & 9 \\ 6 & 5 \end{bmatrix}$

13. Find QY. Show your work.

14. Which expression is equal to $(12a) + (12b)$?

A. $12ab$
B. $12(a + b)$
C. $(12 \bullet 12) + (a \bullet b)$
D. $(12 + 12) \bullet (a + b)$

15. You want to fly from Boston to Davenport to visit your Aunt Robyn. The airline you have chosen has the following transportation route network from Boston to Davenport.

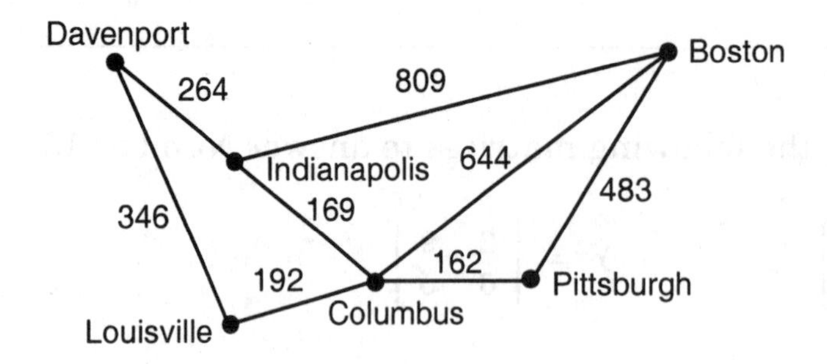

A. If the only thing you are concerned about is flying the least amount of miles, what would be the best traceable path from Boston to Davenport?

____

____

B. If mileage is not a concern, list another possible traceable path from Boston to Davenport.

____

____

C. What might be some other considerations you might want to include in choosing the best traceable path from Boston to Davenport?

____

____

16. Which **inverse operation** needs to be performed on $\frac{w}{13}$ so that the variable stands alone?

A. division
B. addition
C. subtraction
D. multiplication

17. Which does **not** express the number 150?

A. $\sqrt{22,225}$

B. $|{}^{-}150|$

C. $2 \bullet 3 \bullet 5^2$

D. $\frac{300}{2}$

18. The temperature on Friday was 9 degrees cooler than Thursday's temperature of 74 degrees. If Saturday's temperature is 25 degrees warmer than Friday's temperature, what is the temperature on Saturday?

A. 108°
B. 99°
C. 90°
D. 65°

19. Vicki is raising money for a charity. Her goal is to raise $525.00 from business donations. At the end of two weeks, she has raised 85% of her goal. Which of the following would be a good estimate of how much money she has left to raise in order to meet her goal?

A. $75.00
B. $85.00
C. $210.00
D. $425.00

20. The table below shows the top money-making movies at theaters the past week.

Top Movies—Weekend Box Office Gross*

Supercat	$12.5
Technocop	$8.2
Delusional Tendencies	$3.0
Airforce Commandos	$ .3
Promises and Lies	$ .3

***Figures are in millions**

What is the total box office gross of the 5 movies?

A. $2.43 \bullet 10^2$
B. $24.3 \bullet 10^2$
C. $2.43 \bullet 10^6$
D. $2.43 \bullet 10^7$

Patterns, Relations, and Functions

Lesson 4: Algebra
Lesson 5: Functions
Lesson 6: Trigonometry

Lesson 4: Algebra

There are different ways of expressing algebraic information.

Expression: A symbol and/or number, or set of symbols and/or numbers, representing a mathematical value. The symbols and/or numbers may be connected by signs of operations or inequalities.

$2x^3 + 4$ $5x - 6$ $\frac{2}{1} \geq x$

$3 > 1$ $^-4 < {}^-1$

Equation: A mathematical sentence that shows that two expressions are equal.

$2x + 5 = 17$ $\frac{2x}{10} = 40$ $^-8 - 10 = {}^-18$

Inequality: A mathematical sentence that shows that two expressions are not equal.

$2 < 5$ $^-3 > {}^-10$ $2 \neq 6$

Variables: Place holders for numbers whose values are unknown. Variables are represented by letters.

$\boldsymbol{y} = 3\boldsymbol{x} + 2$ $2\boldsymbol{a} - 8 = 6$ $\boldsymbol{V} = \frac{4}{3}\pi \boldsymbol{r}^3$

$12\boldsymbol{x} - 10$ $\frac{\boldsymbol{m}}{3} = 15$ $8 \geq \boldsymbol{x} > 2$

Coefficients: Numbers that are in front of variables.

$y = \mathbf{3}x + 2$ $\mathbf{2}a - 8 = 6$ $v = \mathbf{\frac{4}{3}}\pi r^3$

Constants: Numbers that stand alone.

$y = 3x + \mathbf{2}$ $2a - \mathbf{8} = \mathbf{6}$ $x = \mathbf{34}$

Solving Equations with Variables

To solve an equation that contains a variable, you isolate the variable using inverse operations.

Practice

Directions: Solve and check for Numbers 1 through 6.

1. $4w + 2 = 26$ $w =$ ____________

2. $42 - k = 51$ $k =$ ____________

3. $x - \frac{3}{10} = \frac{2}{5}$ $x =$ ____________

4. $14 + b = 52$ $b =$ ____________

5. $\frac{m}{5} + 18 = 14$ $m =$ ____________

6. $2 - 7z = \frac{5}{6}$ $z =$ ____________

Inequalities

The examples below are all inequalities.

$x \geq 3$ $y < x^2$ $5w \neq 100$

The relationship between inequalities is shown by one of the following symbols.

$<$ less than $>$ greater than

$\leq$ less than or equal to $\geq$ greater than or equal to

$\neq$ not equal to

Graphing Inequalities on a Number Line

Inequalities can be graphed on a number line.

Example

"x is less than 9" can be expressed as $x < 9$ or $9 > x$.

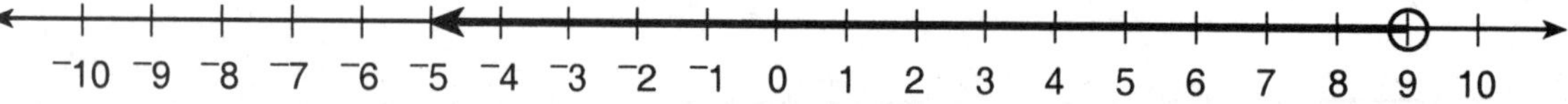

The ○ at 9 shows that 9 is **excluded** from the solution set.

$^{-}2 < n \leq 5$

The number line below shows that n is greater than $^{-}2$ and less than or equal to 5.

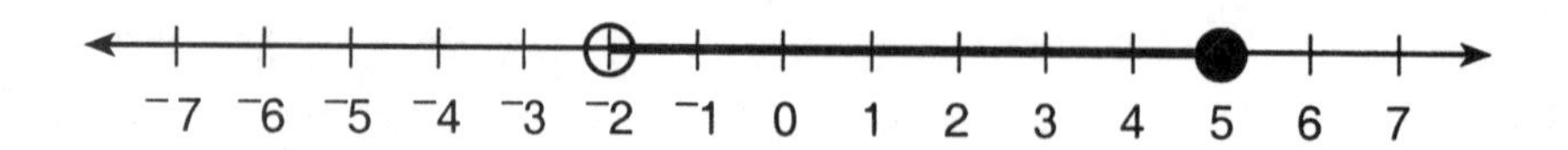

The ● at 5 shows that 5 is **included** in the solution set. The ○ at $^{-}2$ means $^{-}2$ is **excluded** from the solution set.

Practice

Directions: Write an inequality for each expression. Then graph each inequality.

1. R is greater than or equal to $^{-}1.5$ ____________________

2. g is less than 20 ____________________

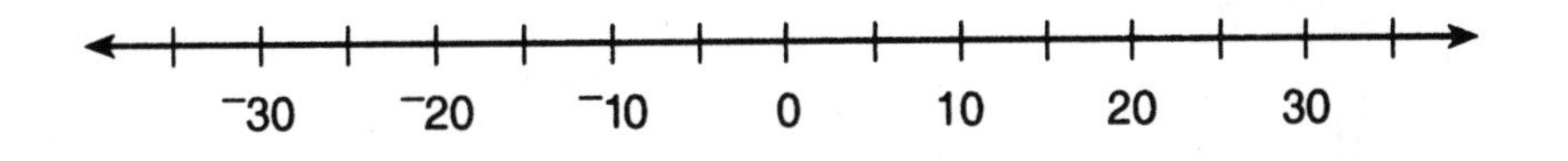

Directions: Write the expression for the inequality described by each graph. Use x for the variable.

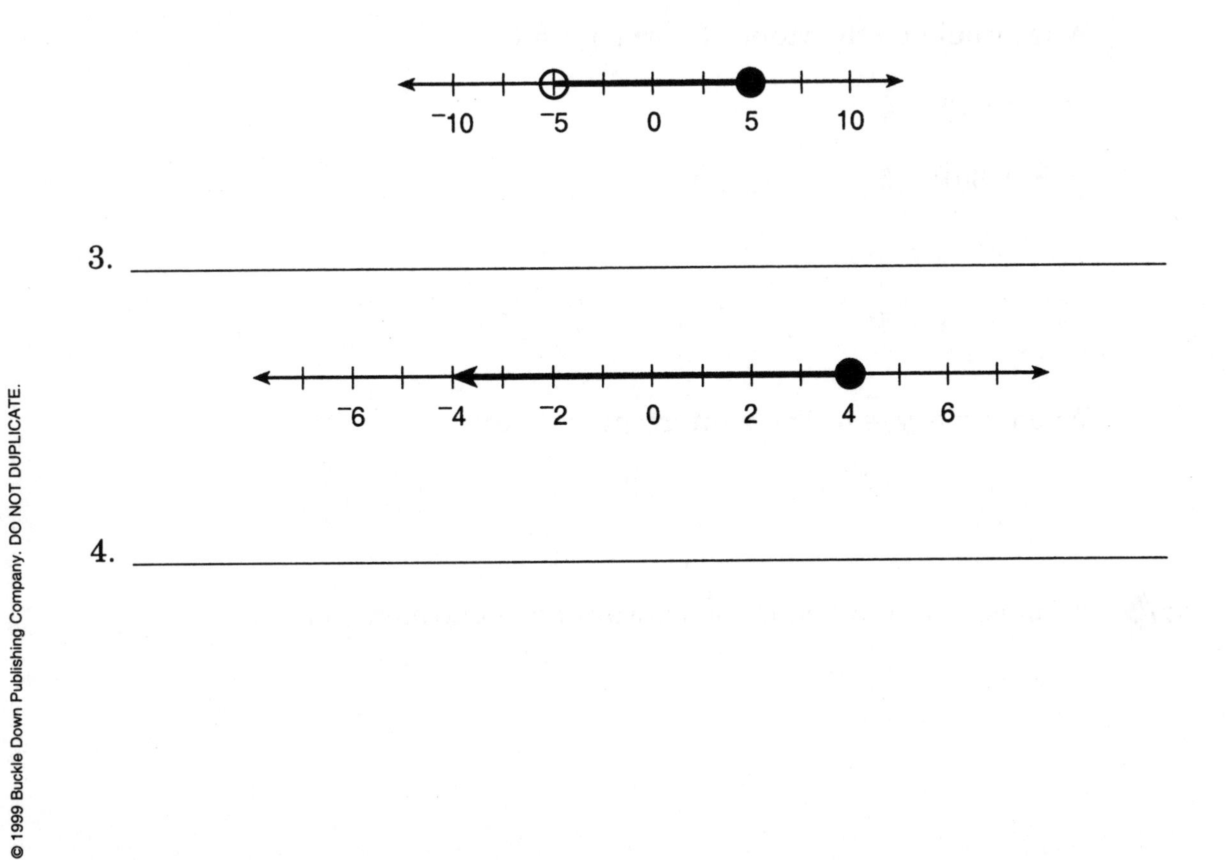

3. ____________________

4. ____________________

Graphing a Linear Equation

To graph a line, you need at least two points. The ordered pair (2, 1) is one solution to the linear equation $x + 3y = 5$. How could you find a second point?

You can assign values to x and/or y, and solve the equation to see if those values make the equation true. It is easier if you first assign a value of 0 to x and then to y. This is called finding the x- and y-intercepts.

Example

What would be the value of y when $x = 0$?

$$x + 3y = 5$$
$$0 + 3y = 5$$
$$3y = 5$$
$$\frac{3y}{3} = \frac{5}{3}$$
$$y = 1\frac{2}{3}$$

When $x = 0$, $y = 1\frac{2}{3}$. The y-intercept is $(0, 1\frac{2}{3})$.

What would be the value of x when $y = 0$?

$$x + 3y = 5$$
$$x + 3(0) = 5$$
$$x + 0 = 5$$
$$x = 5$$

When $x = 5$, $y = 0$. The x-intercept is (5, 0).

Variables in linear equations always have exponents of 1.

Practice

1. Graph the linear equation $x + 3y = 5$. Use the points given on page 40.

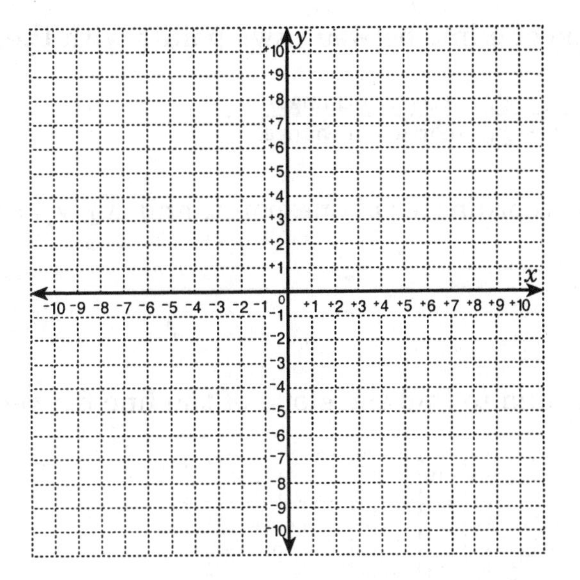

2. Complete the table and graph the equation $2x - y = 4$.

x	y
	0
0	-4
	2

3. Circle the linear equation.

$y = 3x^2 + 6$ $\qquad$ $y - 2x = 5$ $\qquad$ $x^2 + y^2 = 4$

Slope

The **slope** of a line describes how steep the change is as you follow the line from left to right.

You can find the slope of a line between two points with the formula

$$\text{slope} = \frac{y_2 - y_1}{x_2 - x_1} \quad \frac{\text{(vertical change)}}{\text{(horizontal change)}}$$

where (x_1, y_1) are the coordinates of one point, and (x_2, y_2) are the coordinates of the other point.

Example

Use the formula to find the slope of the line between points A and D.

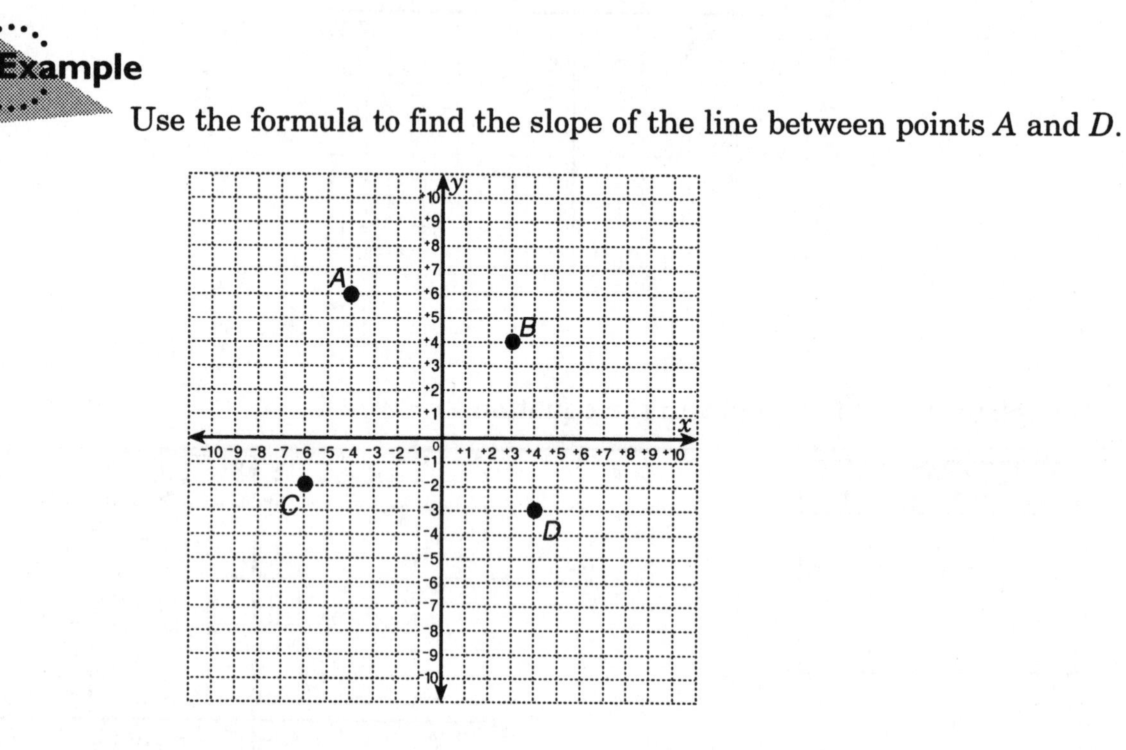

$(^-4, 6)$ and $(4, ^-3)$

$x_1 \; y_1 \qquad x_2 \; y_2$

$$\text{Slope} = \frac{y_2 - y_1}{x_2 - x_1}$$

$$= \frac{^-3 - 6}{4 - (^-4)}$$

$$= \frac{^-9}{8}$$

Practice

Directions: Find the slope of the line between each pair of points.

1. *A* and *B*
2. *A* and C
3. *B* and *C*
4. *B* and *D*

A line has a **positive slope** when it rises from left to right and has a **negative slope** when it falls from left to right.

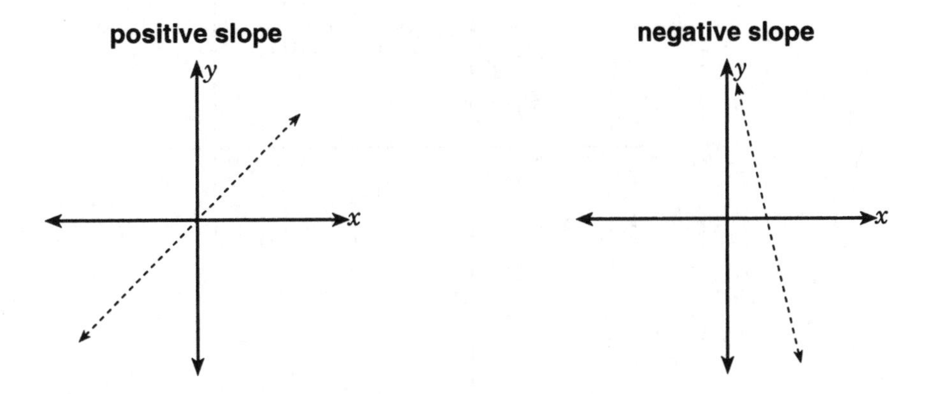

A **horizontal line** is said to have a **slope of zero**; a **vertical line** has an **undefined slope**.

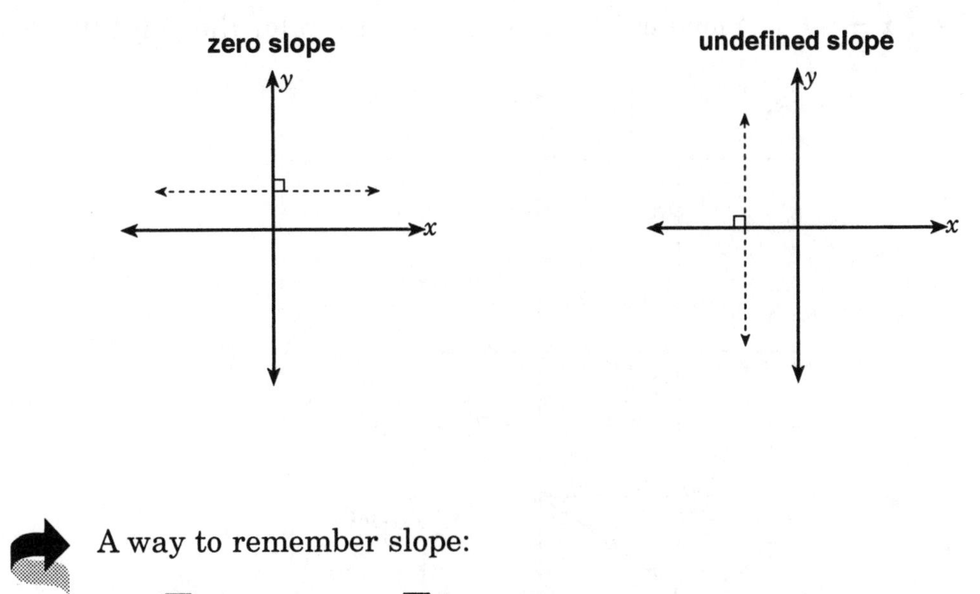

A way to remember slope:

Hori**Z**ontal line has **Z**ero slope.

Using Slope to Graph a Linear Equation

All linear equations can be written in **slope-intercept** form.

$$y = mx + b$$

where m is the slope of the line, b is the y-intercept and x and y are the variables.

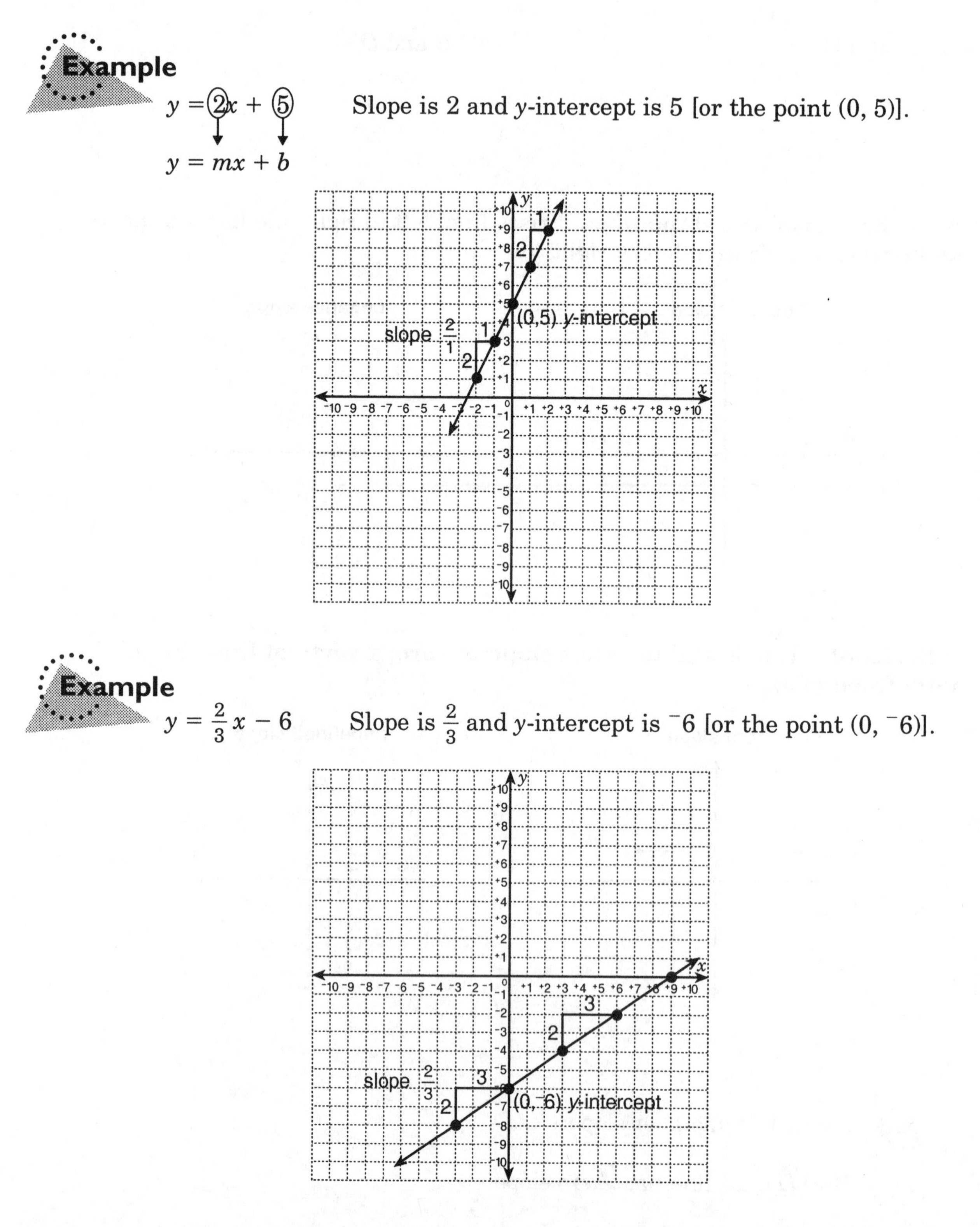

Example

$y = 2x + 5$ → $y = mx + b$ Slope is 2 and y-intercept is 5 [or the point (0, 5)].

Example

$y = \frac{2}{3}x - 6$ Slope is $\frac{2}{3}$ and y-intercept is $^{-}6$ [or the point (0, $^{-}6$)].

Practice

Directions: Identify and then use the slope and y-intercept to graph the equations in Numbers 1 and 2.

1. $y = -\frac{2}{3}x + 8$

   $m =$ ______

   $b =$ ______

y
+10 +9 +8 +7 +6 +5 +4 +3 +2 +1
x
−10 −9 −8 −7 −6 −5 −4 −3 −2 −1 0 +1 +2 +3 +4 +5 +6 +7 +8 +9 +10
−1 −2 −3 −4 −5 −6 −7 −8 −9 −10

2. $y - 5x = 1$

   $m =$ ______

   $b =$ ______

y
+10 +9 +8 +7 +6 +5 +4 +3 +2 +1
x
−10 −9 −8 −7 −6 −5 −4 −3 −2 −1 0 +1 +2 +3 +4 +5 +6 +7 +8 +9 +10
−1 −2 −3 −4 −5 −6 −7 −8 −9 −10

Directions: Identify the slope of the graphs in Numbers 3 and 4.

3. slope = ______________

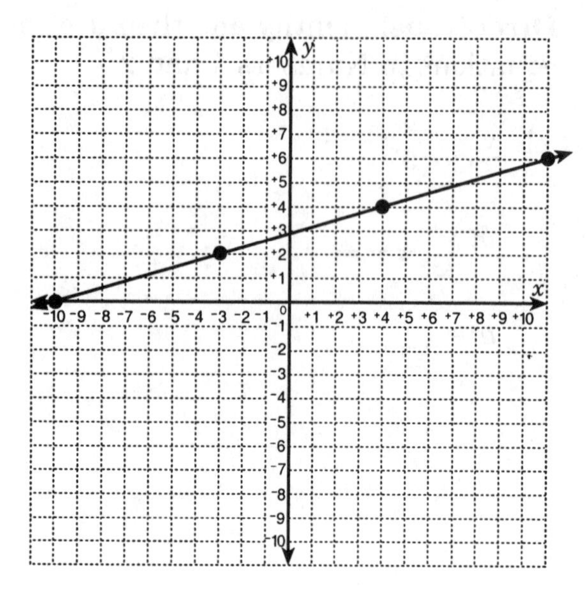

4. slope = ______________

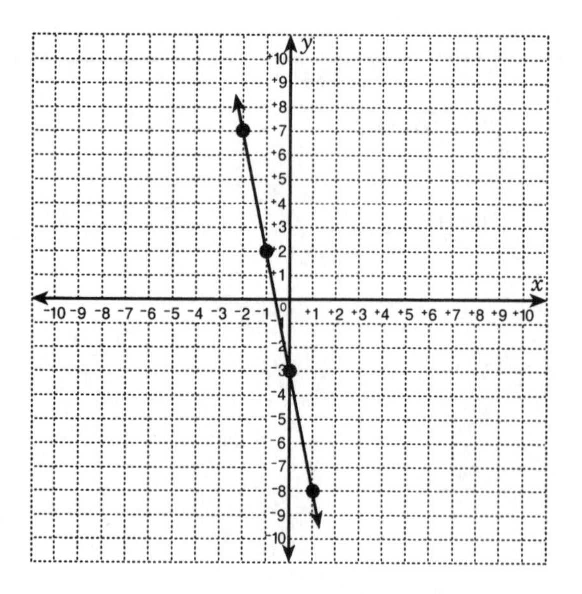

5. Write an equation for a line whose slope is $\frac{5}{4}$ and y-intercept is $^{-}11$.

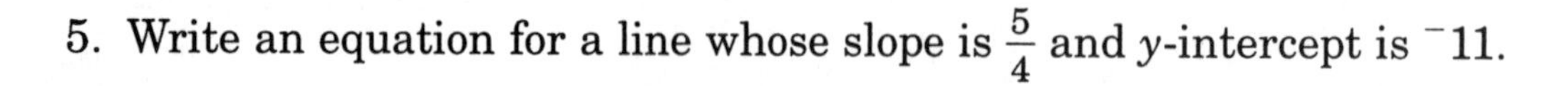

Graphing Linear Inequalities on a Coordinate Plane

The graphs of inequalities are shown by shading.

Example

Graph the inequality: $2x + 3y < 6$.

Step 1: **Replace the inequality symbol with an equal sign.**

$2x + 3y < 6$

$2x + 3y = 6$

Step 2: **Set up a table of values.**

To create a line, you need at least two points. It is a good idea to choose at least three points for your table. (You can always choose more if you want to.)

$2x + 3y = 6$

$2(0) + 3y = 6 \rightarrow$

$2(3) + 3y = 6 \rightarrow$

$2(^{-}3) + 3y = 6 \rightarrow$

x	*y*
0	2
3	0
⁻3	4

Step 3: **Draw the graph and connect the points.**

The graph is drawn on the next page.

The lines connecting the points will be - - - - - (dotted) because of the < symbol used in the linear inequality.

$2x + 3y < 6$

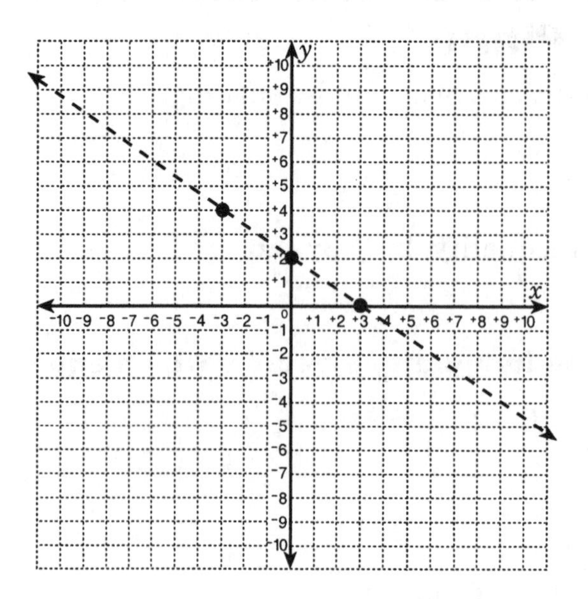

Step 4: **Select a test point.**

A **test point** is any ordered pair that is on either side of the straight line in the graph.

Using (0, 0) is a good idea if it's not on the line.

Substitute the values for x and y in the inequality.

$2x + 3y < 6$

$2(0) + 3(0) < 6$

$0 + 0 < 6$

$0 < 6$

Since 0 is less than 6, the test point (0, 0) has made the inequality true.

Step 5: **Shade in the side of the line that satisfies the inequality.**

If the **test point** makes the inequality **true**, shade the side of the line where the test point is.

If the **test point** makes the inequality **false**, shade the side of the line opposite the test point.

In this example, shade below the dotted line.

Solving Systems

In this section, we will review systems of linear equations and linear inequalities.

Systems of linear equations

Below is an example of a system of linear equations.

$$y = x + 5$$

$$y = 2x + 4$$

When two lines are graphed, three situations are possible.

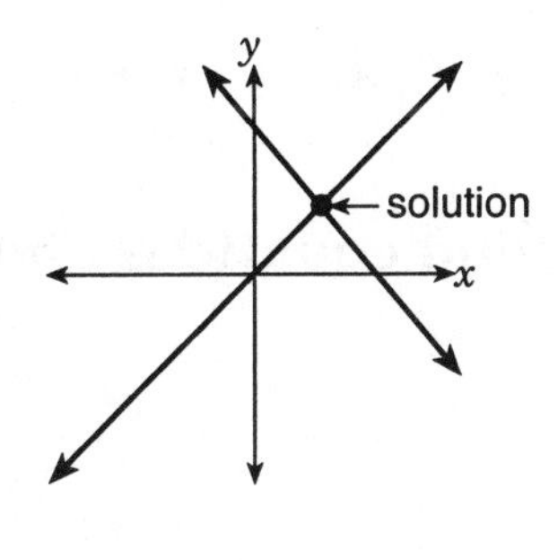

Exactly 1 solution
(Non-parallel lines)

Consistent system

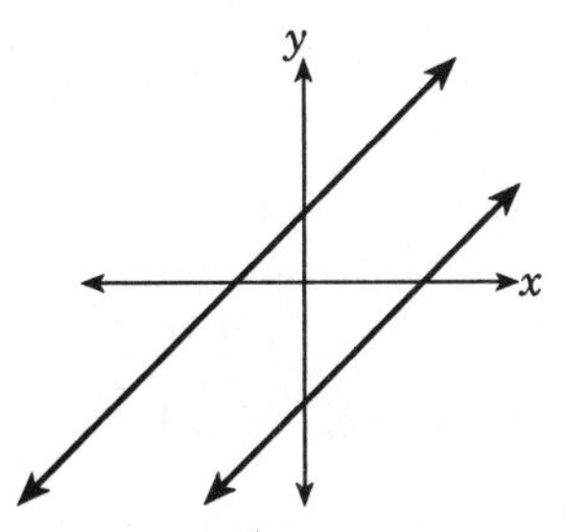

No solution
(Parallel lines)

Inconsistent system

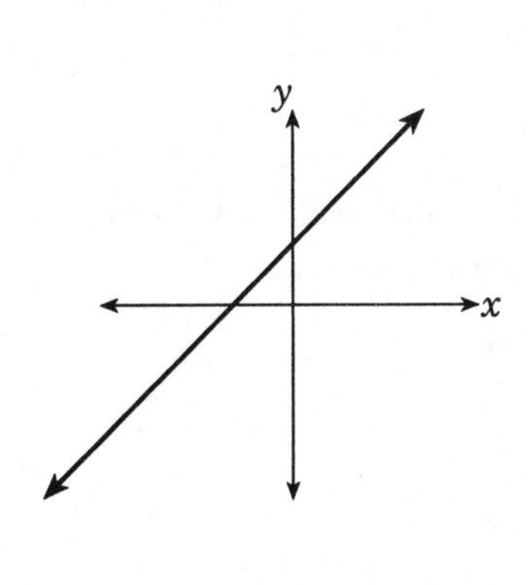

Infinite number of solutions
(Same line)

Dependent system

Example

Solve the following system of equations graphically.

$2x + y = 8$

$x + 3y = 9$

Step 1: **Use the slope-intercept form to graph each line.**

$2x + y = 8$	$x + 3y = 9$
$y = ^{-}2x + 8$	$y = \frac{-1}{3}x + 3$
slope: $= \frac{-2}{1}$	slope: $\frac{-1}{3}$
y-intercept: (0, 8)	y-intercept: (0, 3)

Step 2: **Graph the ordered pairs of the first and second equations and connect the points.**

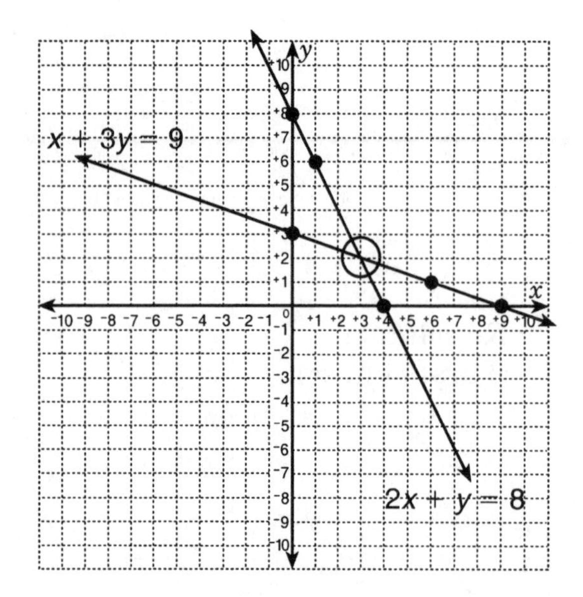

Step 3: **Find the point that satisfies both equations.**

The lines intersect at the point (3, 2). Substitute the values into both original equations to see if they give you true statements.

$2x + y = 8$	$x + 3y = 9$
$2(3) + 2 = 8$	$3 + 3(2) = 9$
$6 + 2 = 8$	$3 + 6 = 9$
$8 = 8$	$9 = 9$

The solution is (3, 2).

Systems of linear inequalities

Example

Solve the following system of inequalities graphically.

$2x + 3y < 6$

$4x - 2y \geq 8$

Step 1: **Replace the inequality symbol with an equal sign (=).**

$2x + 3y < 6$	$4x - 2y \geq 8$
$2x + 3y = 6$	$4x - 2y = 8$

Step 2: **Use slope-intercept form to graph each line.**

$2x + 3y = 6$	$4x - 2y = 8$
$y = \frac{^-2}{3}x + 2$	$y = 2x - 4$
slope: $\frac{^-2}{3}$	slope: $\frac{2}{1}$
y-intercept: (0, 2)	y-intercept: $(0, {}^-4)$

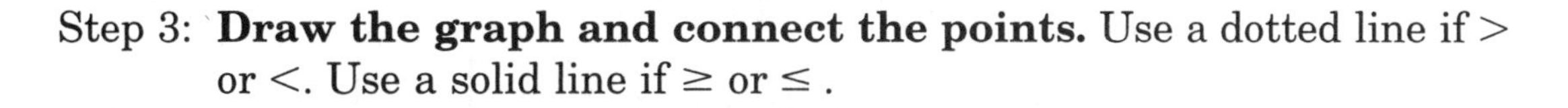

Step 3: **Draw the graph and connect the points.** Use a dotted line if > or <. Use a solid line if ≥ or ≤ .

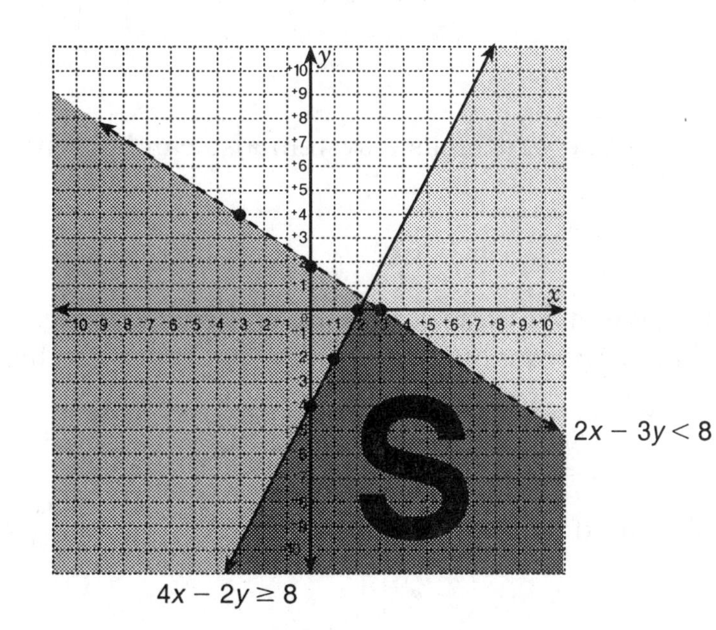

Step 4: **Select a test point for each inequality. Again, we recommend (0, 0).**

The test points for each inequality have been done for you.

$2x + 3y < 6$ $4x - 2y \geq 8$

$0 < 6$ TRUE $0 \geq 8$ FALSE

Step 5: **Shade in the side of the line that satisfies each inequality.**

If the **test point** makes the inequality **true**, shade the side of the line where the test point is.

If the **test point** makes the inequality **false**, shade the side of the line opposite the test point.

The **solution** is the **set of points** that satisfies both of the inequalities. These points are in the area where the shadings overlap, indicated by **S** on the graph.

Systems using matrices

A system also can be represented by matrices. The first matrix consists only of coefficients, the second matrix consists only of variables, and the third matrix consists only of constants. For example, this system

$$\begin{cases} x + 4y = 8 \\ 3x + 5y = 3 \end{cases}$$

is represented by these matrices $\begin{bmatrix} 1 & 4 \\ 3 & 5 \end{bmatrix} \begin{bmatrix} x \\ y \end{bmatrix} = \begin{bmatrix} 8 \\ 3 \end{bmatrix}$

A word problem that can be written as a system also can be written in matrix form.

Example

Joni has a total of 34 coins consisting of dimes and nickels. The total value is \$1.90. How many dimes and nickels does she have?

$$\begin{cases} x + y = 34 \\ 0.05x + 0.10y = 1.90 \end{cases}$$

is represented by these matrices $\begin{bmatrix} 1 & 1 \\ .05 & .10 \end{bmatrix} \begin{bmatrix} x \\ y \end{bmatrix} = \begin{bmatrix} 34 \\ 1.90 \end{bmatrix}$

Formulating Equations/Inequalities

Translating a word problem into a mathematical sentence is the heart of problem solving. Often a problem is simple enough that you can make an intuitive leap to the solution without stating the problem mathematically. However, many problems require a combination of intuition and math skills. English needs to be translated into math.

Example

Emily has arranged her rock collection for the upcoming gem and mineral show. She has half as many pieces of carnelian as she has of jasper, and she has 5 more smoky quartz rocks than carnelian. She has a total of 57 rocks. Find the number of pieces of jasper (n) she has.

Step 1: **List what you know.**

Let n = the number of pieces of jasper

The number of pieces of carnelian = jasper $\div 2 = \frac{n}{2}$

The number of pieces of smoky quartz = 5 + carnelian = $5 + \frac{n}{2}$

The number of pieces of jasper + carnelian + smoky quartz = 57

Step 2: **Substitute the numerical expressions you found into your original equation.**

jasper + carnelian + smoky quartz = 57

↑ ↑ ↑

$$n \quad + \quad \frac{n}{2} \quad + \quad 5 + \frac{n}{2} \quad = 57$$

Step 3: **Solve the equation.**

$$n + \frac{n}{2} + (5 + \frac{n}{2}) = 57$$

$$n + \frac{(n + n)}{2} = 57 - 5$$

$$n + \frac{(n + n)}{2} = 52$$

$$n + \frac{2n}{2} = 52$$

$$n + n = 52$$

$$2n = 52$$

$$n = 26$$

There are 26 pieces of jasper.

Step 4: **Check your answer.**

Substitute the value of n back into the original equation to check your work.

$$26 + \frac{26}{2} + (5 + \frac{26}{2}) = 57$$

$$26 + 13 + 18 = 57$$

$$57 = 57$$

Example

A medical study was conducted at a university concerning people's weight gains or losses on a certain diet. Subjects selected for the study had to weigh between 140 lb and 210 lb. If n represents weight, what sentence expresses this weight requirement?

Step 1: **List what you know.**

Subject's weight should be greater than or equal to 140 lb.

Subject's weight should be less than or equal to 210 lb.

Step 2: **Make a mathematical translation of each statement.**

$$\left.\begin{array}{l} n \geq 140 \\ n \leq 210 \end{array}\right\} n \text{ is between 140 and 210.}$$

Step 3: **Combine the two expressions to form a double inequality.**

$140 \leq n \leq 210$ or $210 \geq n \geq 140$

Both inequality signs must be going in the same direction in a double inequality.

Step 4: **Check your answer.**

Since it is fairly easy to mix up the signs, check your inequality. Do you have two true statements?

$140 \leq n$ True

$n \leq 210$ True

1. At The Salad Palace, salads are \$2.59 plus \$0.20 per ounce for any salad over 8 oz. Write an equation that would give the extra weight n (weight over 8 oz) of a salad that costs \$4.99.

___

2. Ethan's age is 8 years more than twice the age of his niece Laurie. Ethan is also $\frac{2}{3}$ the age of his Uncle Matt. Uncle Matt is 27 years old. Write an equation that would give the age n of Laurie.

___

3. For a certain job on an assembly line, it was suggested that workers with a maximum height of 73 in. and a minimum height of 62 in. would be best suited for the work. Write an inequality that expresses this range. Use n for worker's height.

___

4. Ticket prices for the school play are listed below:

Senior Citizens (age 65 and older)	\$2.00
Adults (ages 18–64)	\$6.00
Children (ages 17 and younger)	\$3.00

\$800 worth of tickets were sold for Friday's showing of the play. Ninety tickets were purchased at adult prices, and 60 tickets were purchased at children's prices.

Write an equation that shows how many tickets were purchased at senior citizens' prices for Friday's show. Use t for the unknown number of tickets.

___

Manipulating Equations

Use inverse operations to manipulate an equation or formula and solve for a specified variable. Treat all the variables, except the one you are solving for, as constants.

Example

The formula $f = \frac{l}{d}$ tells how to calculate a camera's f-stop. In this formula, f represents the f-stop, l represents the approximate distance from the lens to the film, and d represents the diameter of the lens. Solve the formula for d.

$$f = \frac{l}{d}$$

$$\boldsymbol{d}f = \left(\frac{l}{d}\right)\boldsymbol{d}$$ Multiply by d on both sides of the equation.

$$df = l$$

$$\frac{df}{\boldsymbol{f}} = \frac{l}{\boldsymbol{f}}$$ Divide by f on both sides of the equation.

$$d = \frac{l}{f}$$

Example

Solve the equation $y = mx + b$ for m.

$$y - \boldsymbol{b} = mx + b - \boldsymbol{b}$$ Subtract b from both sides of the operation.

$$y - b = mx$$

$$\frac{y - b}{\boldsymbol{x}} = \frac{mx}{\boldsymbol{x}}$$ Divide both sides of the equation by x.

$$\frac{y - b}{x} = m$$

1. Solve the equation $\frac{a}{b} = \frac{c}{d}$ for the variable a.

2. Solve the equation $\frac{a}{b} = \frac{c}{d}$ for the variable b.

3. Solve the equation $P = \frac{A}{(1 + r)}$ for the variable r.

Extrapolation/Interpolation

Sometimes you may want to use tables or graphs to find an unknown value. When you make a prediction by **extending** the table or graph, this is called **extrapolation**. When you find an unknown value **between** values you already know, this is called **interpolation**.

Example

This summer, Thomas plans to mow lawns in his neighborhood to earn money for a new pair of rollerblades.

The relationship between the hours he worked and the money he earned is shown in the table below:

Hours Worked	Money Earned
1	\$5.95
2	\$11.90
3	\$17.85
4	\$23.80

This relationship also can be expressed as a graph. The number of hours worked will be on the x-axis, and the money earned in dollars will be on the y-axis.

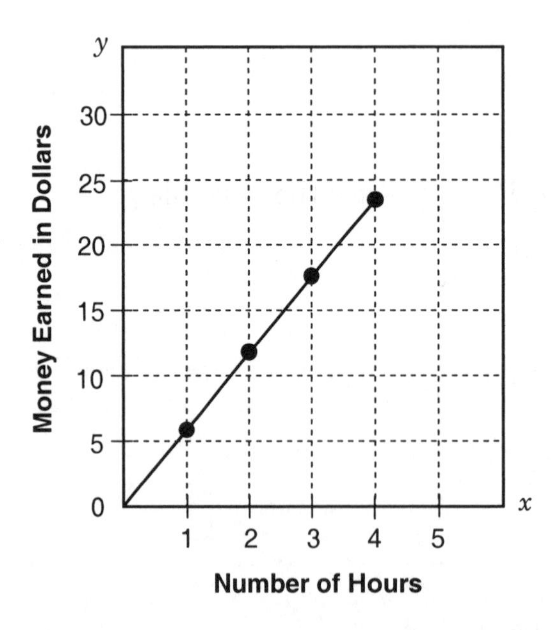

If you use extrapolation and extend the graph, you might predict that Thomas will earn about \$30.00 for 5 hours of work. Using interpolation, you might read between the points for 2 and 3 hours and estimate that Thomas will earn approximately \$15.00 for about $2\frac{1}{2}$ hours work.

Directions: Use the graph from the previous example to answer Numbers 1 through 3.

1. Interpolate to estimate about how many hours Thomas would need to mow to earn about $20.00.

   ____

2. Interpolate to estimate about how much money Thomas would earn after mowing about $1\frac{3}{4}$ hours.

   ____

3. Extrapolate to predict about how much money Thomas would earn after mowing 6 hours.

   ____

Lesson 5: Functions

You use patterns to investigate relationships and to solve problems. Once you find the rule for a pattern, you can describe, extend, or analyze it. You also can use the rule as the basis for creating new patterns.

Number Patterns

To find the rule of number patterns, you need to discover the operation or operations used. In some patterns, the rule is to add; in others, it is to subtract, divide, or multiply. In other patterns, the rule could include a combination of operations.

Examples

Look at the number pattern below.

1	5	9	13	17	21			

Here is a rule that describes this pattern:

Begin with the number 1, then add 4 to it and to each subsequent number.

This is another way to express the rule:

1	5	9	13	17	21

↑ ↑ ↑ ↑ ↑

$1 + 4$ $5 + 4$ $9 + 4$ $13 + 4$ $17 + 4$

Look at the next number pattern.

5	15	45	135	405	1,215

What is the rule of this pattern?

Begin with the number 5, then multiply it and all subsequent numbers by 3.

Here is another way to express the rule:

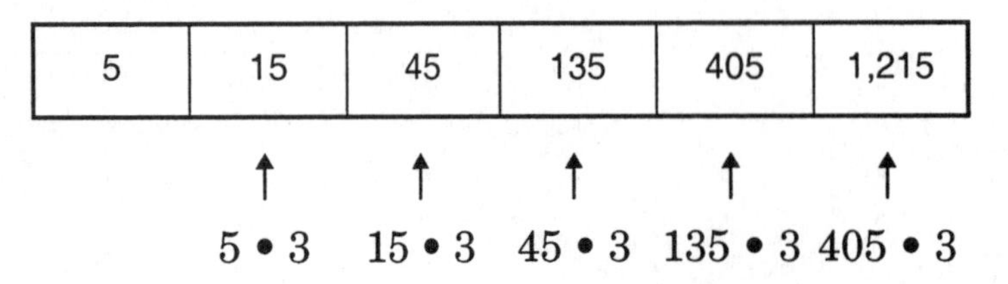

5	15	45	135	405	1,215

Example

Look at one more number pattern. Think about what rule you could use to describe this pattern.

10	11	9	12	8	13

If you need some help, look below.

10	11	9	12	8	13

↑ $10 + 1$ ↑ $11 - 2$ ↑ $9 + 3$ ↑ $12 - 4$ ↑ $8 + 5$

Practice

1. Describe the rule for the pattern above on the lines below.

____

____

____

2. Now extend the pattern three more numbers using the rule you wrote.

10	11	9	12	8	13			

Relations and Functions

A **relation** is any set of ordered pairs. In a relation, different ordered pairs may have the **same first coordinates**.

A **function** is a relation in which different ordered pairs have **different first coordinates**.

The set of first coordinates (usually x values) of the ordered pairs is called the **domain** of a relation. The set of second coordinates (usually y values) is called the **range**.

Functions are presented as tables, graphs, and equations.

Function tables

In a function table, ***n*** represents the **input value** and ***f*(*n*)** the **output value**.

Example

When the input value (n) is equal to 3 and the output value $f(n)$ is equal to $2n$, then $f(n) = 2(3) = 6$.

Complete the table.

n	$f(n)$
3	6
4	8
5	
6	

Notice that $f(n)$ is used to show the output value and not multiplication. $f(n)$ is used to indicate the **value** of f at n.

1. Complete the table for the function $f(n) = 5n - 1$.

n	$f(n) = 5n - 1$
2	9
3	14
4	19
5	
6	

2. The table shows the domain and range of $y = 2x$.

Is each member of the domain matched with only one member of the range?

____

Is $y = 2x$ a relation or a function? ____________

x	y
$^-2$	$^-4$
$^-1$	$^-2$
0	0
1	2
2	4

How to tell when a graph shows a function

The **vertical line test** is a simple test to show if a graph represents a function. If a vertical line intersects two or more points in the graph, the graph does not represent a function.

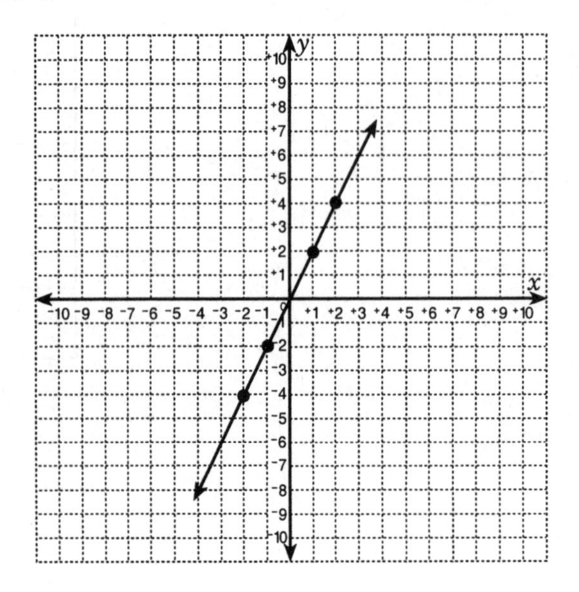

Draw a vertical line on the graph above. (Make sure your vertical line intersects with the original segment.) Is this graph a function? ______________

Practice

Directions: Tell whether the relation is also a function.

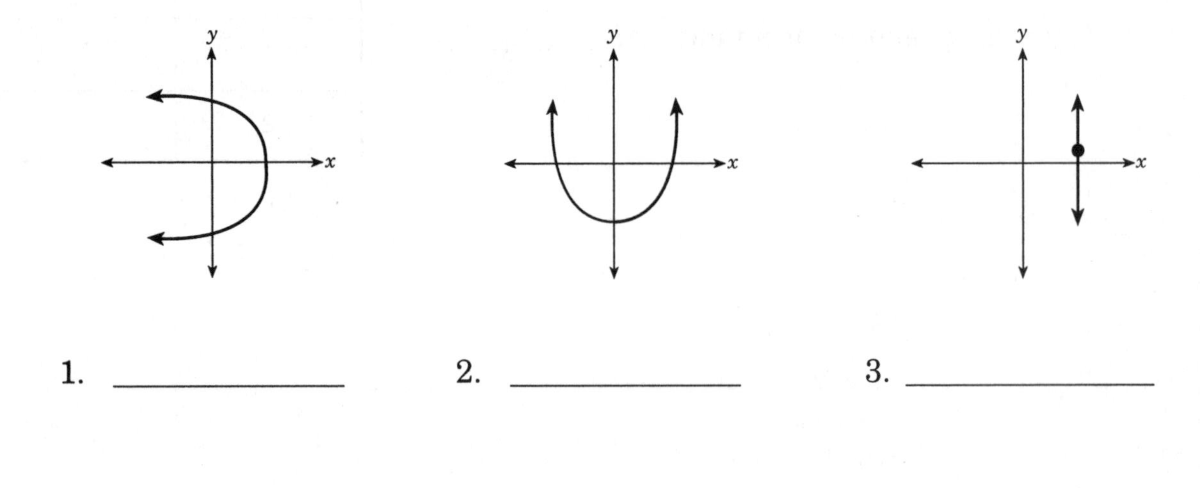

1. ______________ 2. ______________ 3. ______________

All functions are relations but not all relations are functions.

Linear functions

In a linear function, each value of x results in a unique value of y. The variable x must have 1 as its exponent. For example, $y = x^2$ is not a linear function. All of the following are linear functions.

$y = x$ $\quad$ $y = x - 3$ $\quad$ $y = 2x + 5$ $\quad$ $5y = 15x - 10$

Example

Graph the linear function $y - 2x = 5$.

Set up a table of values. Solving the equation for y makes it easier to find values for x.

x	y = 2x + 5	ordered pairs
⁻2	1	(⁻2, 1)
⁻1	3	(⁻1, 3)
0	5	(0, 5)
1	7	(1, 7)
2	9	(2, 9)

As their name suggests, linear functions will form a straight line when graphed.

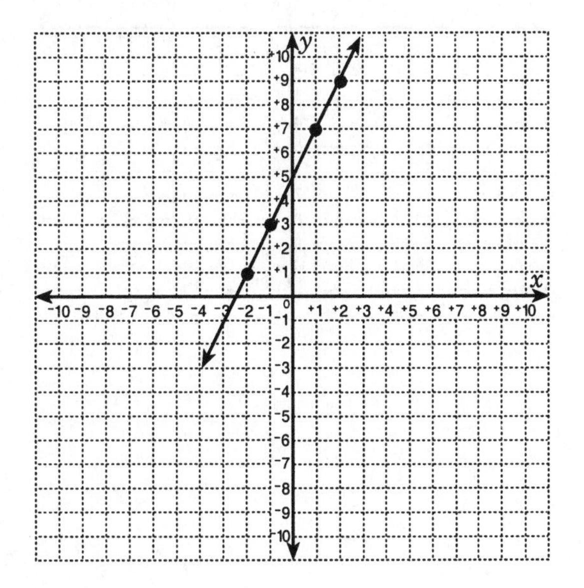

Practice

1. Circle the equation that is a linear function.

$7x + y = 9$ $7x^2 + y = 9$ $x = 9$

2. Solve the linear function $3x + y = 6$ for y. ________________

3. Graph the function in Number 2.

Quadratic functions

A **quadratic equation** is a nonlinear equation and can be written as:

$$ax^2 + bx + c = 0$$

One way of solving quadratic equations is by **factoring**.

Example

$x^2 - 2x = 8$

Step 1: **Set all terms equal to 0.**

$$x^2 - 2x - 8 = 0$$

Step 2: **Factor.**

$$(x - 4)(x + 2) = 0$$

Step 3: **Set each factor equal to 0.**

$x - 4 = 0$ $\qquad$ $x + 2 = 0$

Step 4: **Solve each of these equations.**

$x - 4 = 0$ $\qquad$ $x + 2 = 0$

$x - 4 + 4 = 0 + 4$ $\qquad$ $x + 2 - 2 = 0 - 2$

$x = 4$ $\qquad$ and $\qquad$ $x = {}^{-}2$

Not every quadratic equation can be factored easily and many cannot be factored at all. Another way of solving quadratic equations is by using the **quadratic formula**.

$$x = \frac{{}^{-}b \pm \sqrt{b^2 - 4ac}}{2a} \qquad (a \neq 0)$$

where

a = the coefficient of the squared term

b = the coefficient of the linear term

c = the constant

Example

$2x^2 - 7x = {}^-5$

Step 1: **Set all terms equal to 0.**

$$ax^2 + bx + c = 0$$

$$2x^2 - 7x + 5 = 0$$

Step 2: **Substitute the values for *a*, *b*, and *c* in the quadratic formula.**

$a = 2$ $b = {}^-7$ $c = 5$

$$x = \frac{{}^-b \pm \sqrt{b^2 - 4ac}}{2a}$$

$$x = \frac{{}^-({}^-7) \pm \sqrt{({}^-7)^2 - 4(2)(5)}}{2(2)}$$

Step 3: **Simplify the equation.**

$$x = \frac{7 \pm \sqrt{49 - 40}}{4}$$

$$x = \frac{7 \pm \sqrt{9}}{4}$$

$$x = \frac{7 \pm 3}{4}$$

Step 4: **Solve for (+) and then (–).**

$x = \frac{7 + 3}{4}$ $x = \frac{7 - 3}{4}$

$x = \frac{10}{4}$ $x = \frac{4}{4}$

$x = \frac{5}{2}$ and $x = 1$

Example

Tony has a garden whose length is 5 feet less than twice its width. Find the length and width of Tony's garden if its area is 63 square feet.

Let x = width

$2x - 5$ = length

$$lw = A$$

$$(2x - 5)(x) = 63$$

$$2x^2 - 5x = 63$$

$$2x^2 - 5x - 63 = 0$$

In this equation, $a = 2$, $b = 5$, and $c = 63$.

$$x = \frac{^-b \pm \sqrt{b^2 - 4ac}}{2a}$$

$$x = \frac{^-(^-5) \pm \sqrt{(^-5)^2 - 4(2)(^-63)}}{2(2)}$$

$$x = \frac{5 \pm \sqrt{25 + 504}}{4}$$

$$x = \frac{5 \pm 23}{4}$$

$$x = 7 \text{ and } x = {}^-4.5$$

Since width (and length) can't be negative, choose $x = 7$.

Tony's garden measures 7 ft by 9 ft long.

1. Solve by factoring.

   $x^2 + 8x = {}^{-}7$

2. Solve by using the quadratic formula.

   $3x^2 = {}^{-}8x - 5$

3. The area of a rectangular patio is 24 square meters. Find the length and width of the rectangular patio if its length is 2 meters greater than its width.

   Let x = ______________

length = ______________ width = ______________

Graphing quadratic functions

The graph of a quadratic equation of the form $y = ax^2 + bx + c$ will be a smooth curve called a **parabola**.

If the value of a is **positive**, the parabola will open **upward**. The vertex identifies the **minimum** value of the function.

If the value of a is **negative**, the parabola will open **downward**. The vertex identifies the **maximum** value of the function.

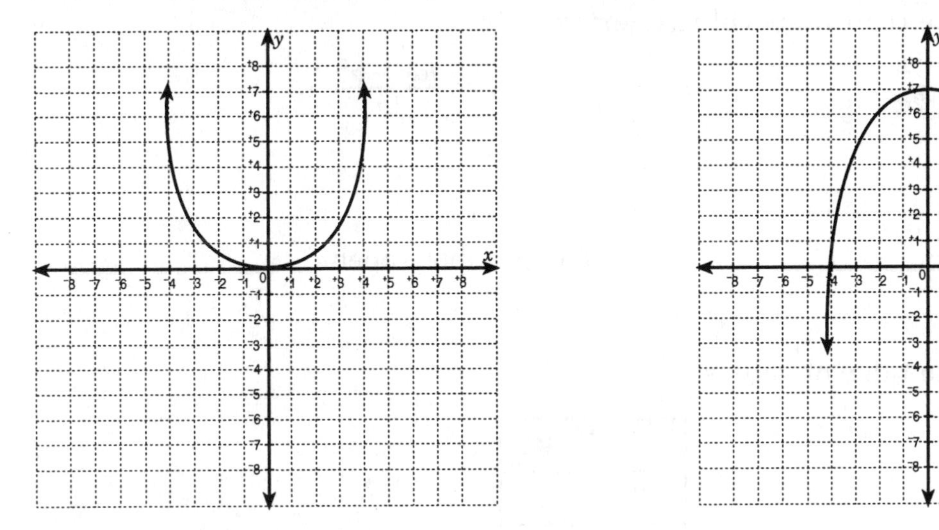

Each parabola has a **vertex** (the highest or lowest point on the curve) and an **axis of symmetry**.

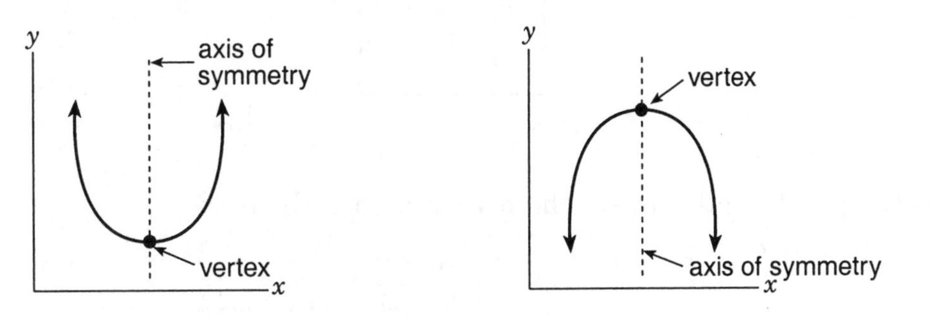

The ***x*-coordinate** of the vertex is found by using

$$x = \frac{^{-}b}{2a}$$

The ***y*-coordinate** of the vertex is found by using

$$y = \frac{4ac - b^2}{4a}$$

Practice

Graph $-2x^2 + 16x - 24 = 0$

1. Determine the numerical value of a, b, and c.

   $a =$ __________ $b =$ __________ $c =$ __________

2. Calculate the coordinates of the vertex.

   $x = \frac{^{-}b}{2a}$ $y = \frac{4ac - b^2}{4a}$

3. Vertex: ______________ The parabola opens ______________

4. Complete the table of values.

x	y
2	
3	
4	
5	
6	

5. Plot the points and connect them with a smooth curve.

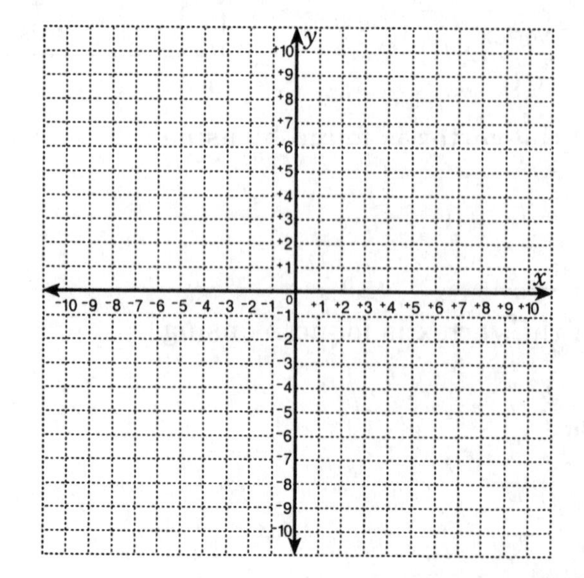

Exponential functions

The equation below shows an exponential function. Its graph is a smooth curve.

$y = 2^x$ ← exponent

↑

base

Example

The amount of money $A(t)$ that the principal of a savings account will be worth after t years, compounded annually, is calculated by an exponential formula.

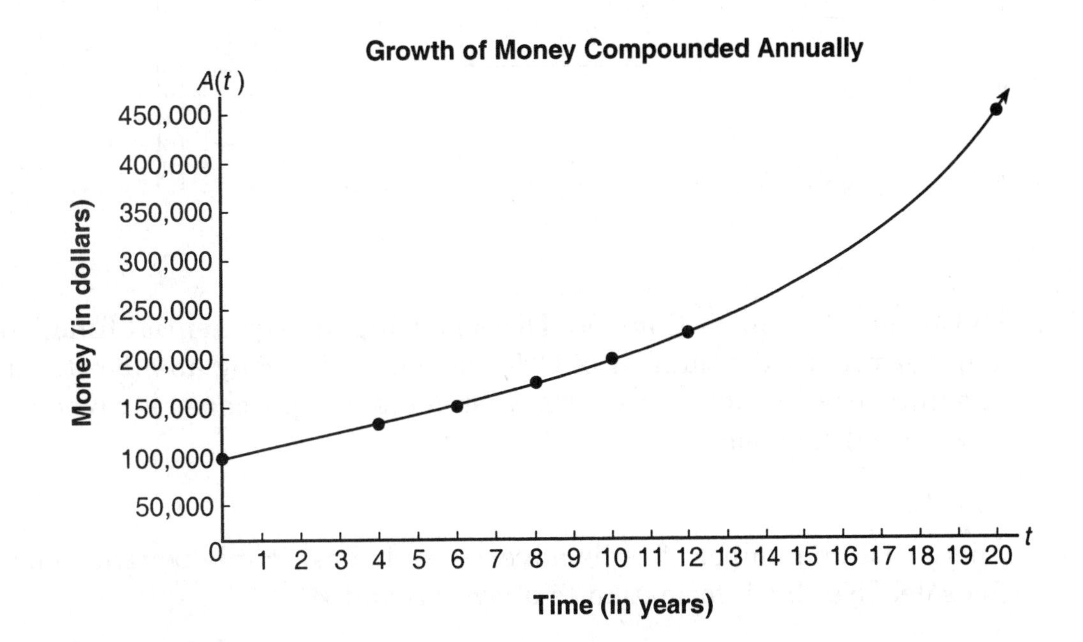

Look at the coordinates of the first point on the graph: (0, 100,000). The first coordinate of this function represents time and the second coordinate represents money.

The account started out with $100,000 in it.

The approximate amount of money in the account after 6 years is $150,000.

Approximately how many years will it take for the account to grow to $200,000? The coordinates (10, 200,000) give you the answer. It will take 10 years.

1. Complete the table and plot the points.

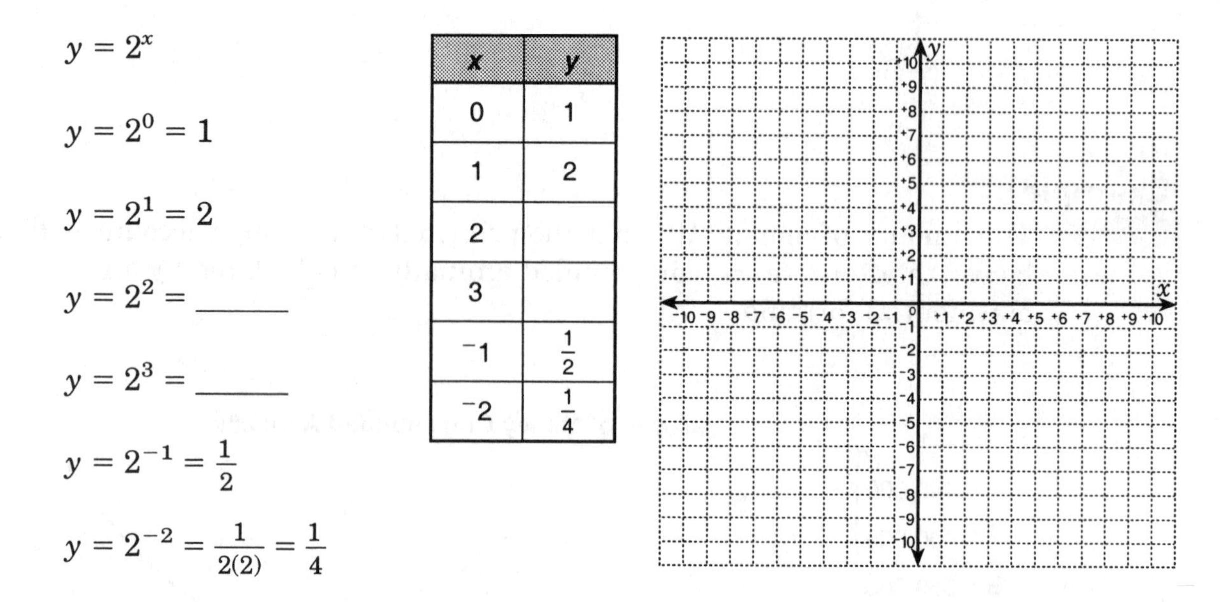

$y = 2^x$

$y = 2^0 = 1$

$y = 2^1 = 2$

$y = 2^2 =$ ______

$y = 2^3 =$ ______

$y = 2^{-1} = \frac{1}{2}$

$y = 2^{-2} = \frac{1}{2(2)} = \frac{1}{4}$

x	y
0	1
1	2
2	
3	
$^-1$	$\frac{1}{2}$
$^-2$	$\frac{1}{4}$

2. The owner of Connie's Compact Discs is using an exponential function to help her predict the number of CDs she will sell during an advertised sale. The number of compact discs $N(t)$ customers will purchase is given by the exponential function

   $N(t) = 4t^3$

   where t is the number of radio advertising hours Connie bought to promote the sale. Use this information to answer A and B.

   A. If Connie advertises on the radio for 3 hours, how many CDs can she expect to sell?

   ____

   B. If Connie increases her advertising time to 4 hours, how many more CDs can she expect to sell?

   ____

Special Investigation: Direct/Inverse Variation

Direct and inverse variations are situations in which a change in one quantity corresponds to a predictable change in the other. A **direct variation** is when **both** quantities **increase (or decrease)** by the same factor.

An **inverse variation** is when **one quantity increases** by a certain factor, and the **other quantity decreases** by that same factor.

Directions: Identify each of the situations in Numbers 1 through 3 as a direct or inverse variation and solve.

1. You have 2 gallons of paint and the directions say it will cover 600 square feet. You have 3,600 square feet to paint. How many more gallons of paint will you need to buy?

   ____

2. It takes 4 hours for 12 people to build a shed. Assume that they all do the same amount of work. How many hours will it take for only 3 people to build the same-sized shed?

   ____

3. Meteorologists have found that 150 cm of snow will melt to 16.8 cm of water. Under the same conditions, how many centimeters of water will result from 200 cm of snow?

   ____

Lesson 6: Trigonometry

The word trigonometry comes from the Greek meaning "triangle measurement." This lesson presents three special relationships that exist for all right triangles.

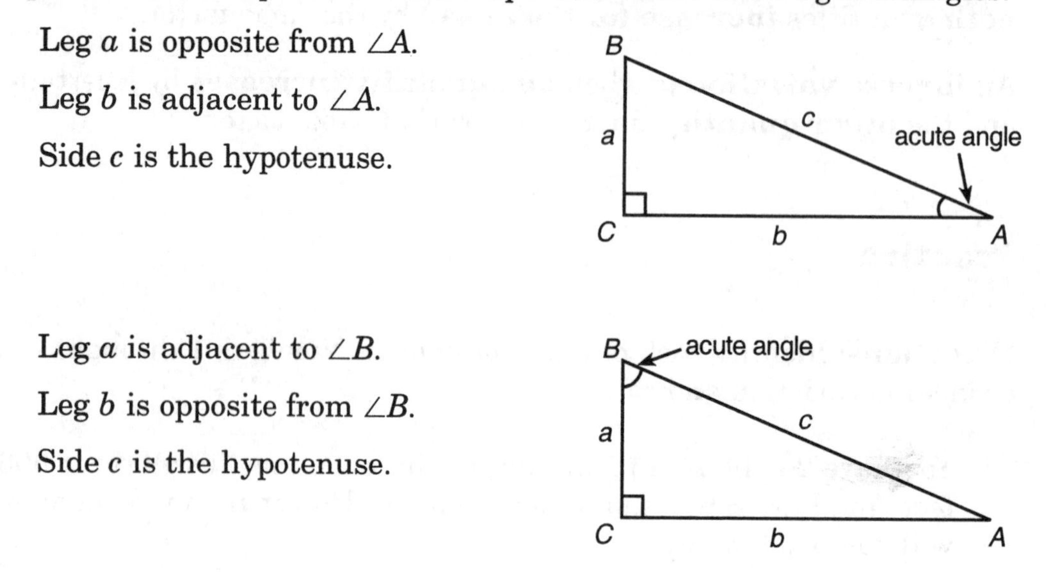

Leg a is opposite from $\angle A$.

Leg b is adjacent to $\angle A$.

Side c is the hypotenuse.

Leg a is adjacent to $\angle B$.

Leg b is opposite from $\angle B$.

Side c is the hypotenuse.

Tangent ratio

The **tangent (tan)** ratio for an acute angle of a right triangle is the ratio of the length of the leg opposite the acute angle to the length of the leg adjacent to the acute angle.

$$\tan A = \frac{\text{length of opposite side}}{\text{length of adjacent side}} = \frac{a}{b}$$

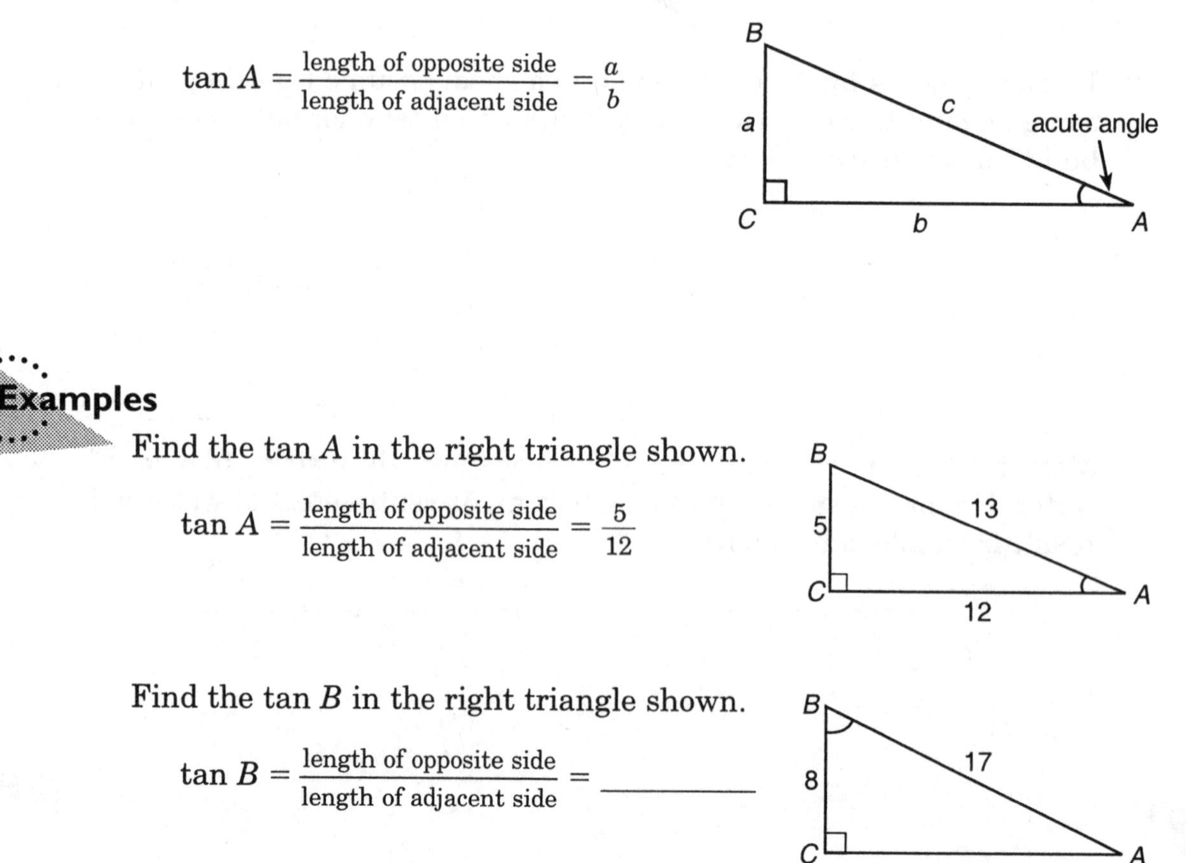

Examples

Find the tan A in the right triangle shown.

$$\tan A = \frac{\text{length of opposite side}}{\text{length of adjacent side}} = \frac{5}{12}$$

Find the tan B in the right triangle shown.

$$\tan B = \frac{\text{length of opposite side}}{\text{length of adjacent side}} = \underline{\hspace{3cm}}$$

Sine ratio

The **sine (sin)** ratio for an acute angle of a right triangle is the ratio of the length of the leg opposite the acute angle to the length of the hypotenuse.

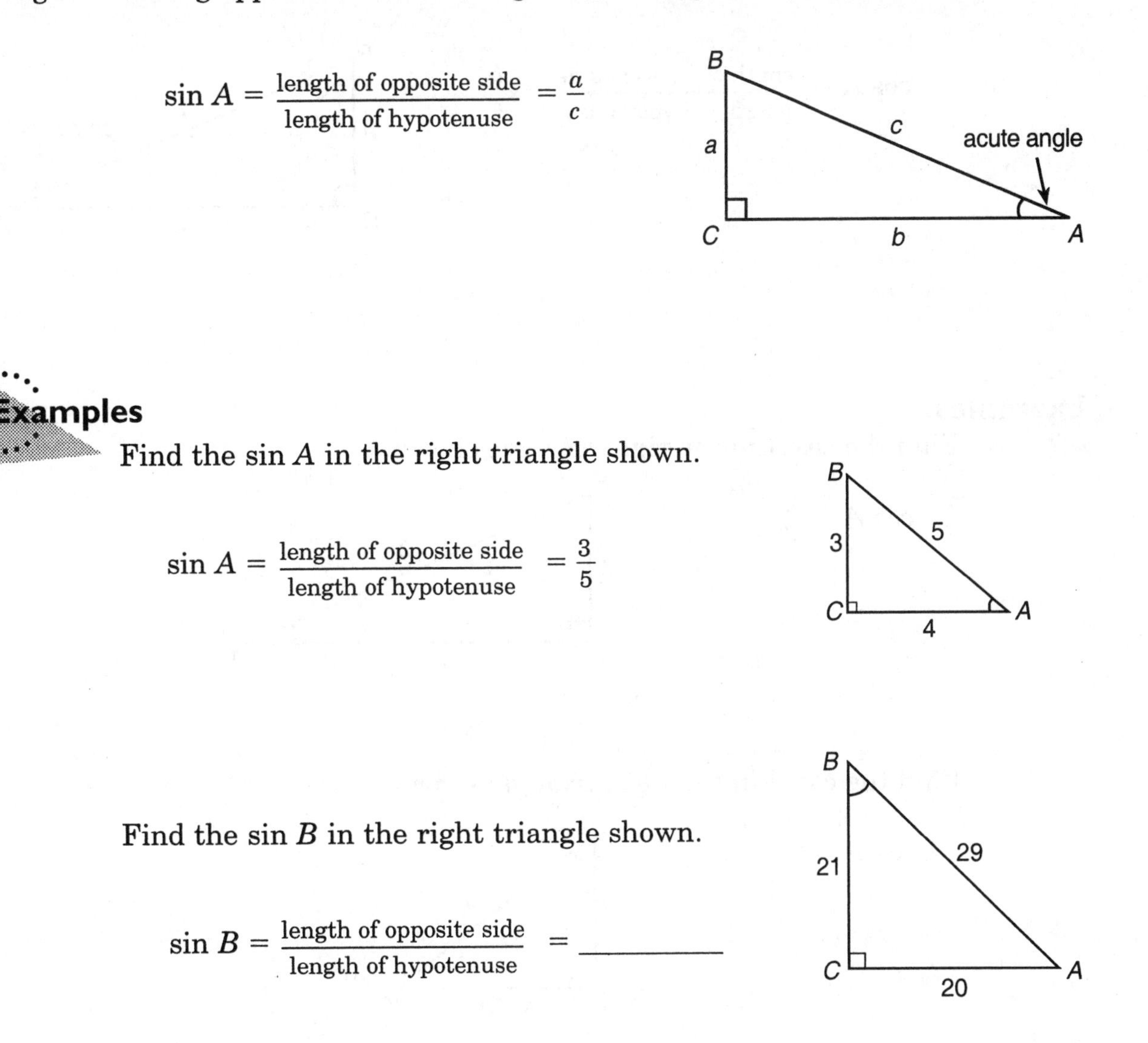

$$\sin A = \frac{\text{length of opposite side}}{\text{length of hypotenuse}} = \frac{a}{c}$$

Examples

Find the sin A in the right triangle shown.

$$\sin A = \frac{\text{length of opposite side}}{\text{length of hypotenuse}} = \frac{3}{5}$$

Find the sin B in the right triangle shown.

$$\sin B = \frac{\text{length of opposite side}}{\text{length of hypotenuse}} = \underline{\qquad\qquad}$$

Cosine ratio

The **cosine (cos)** ratio for an acute angle of a right triangle is the ratio of the length of the leg adjacent to the acute angle to the length of the hypotenuse.

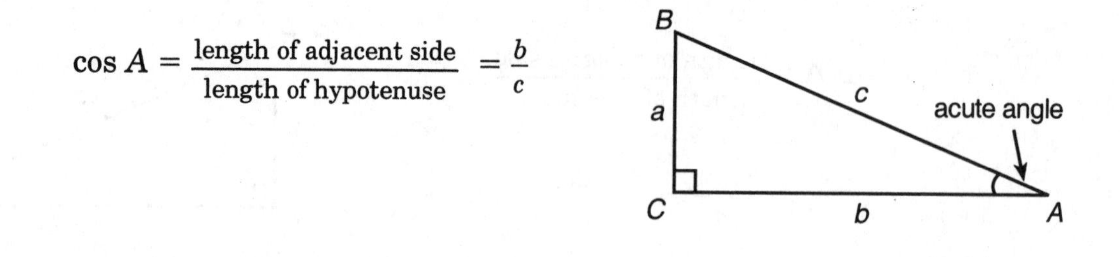

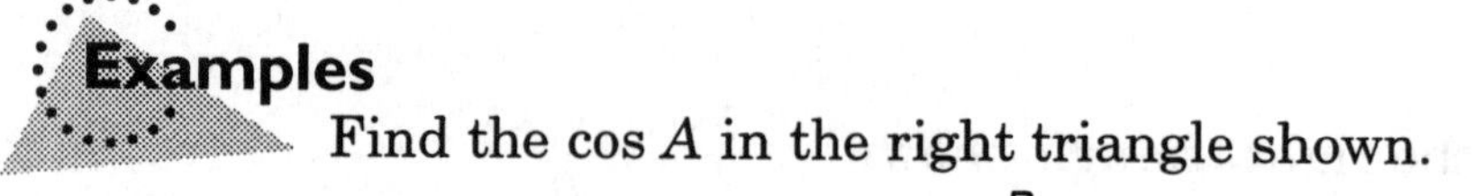

Examples

Find the cos A in the right triangle shown.

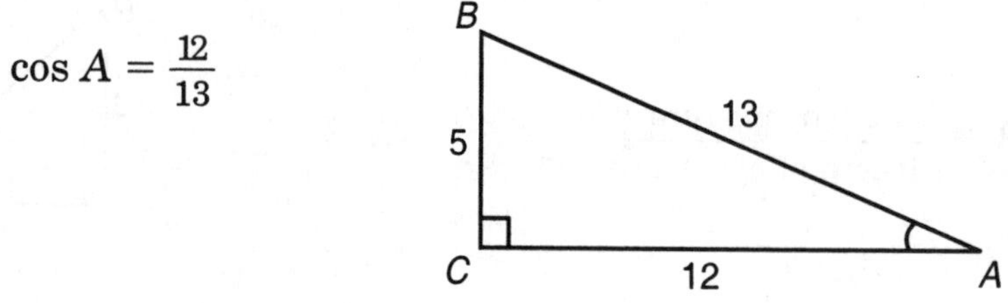

Find the cos B in the right triangle shown.

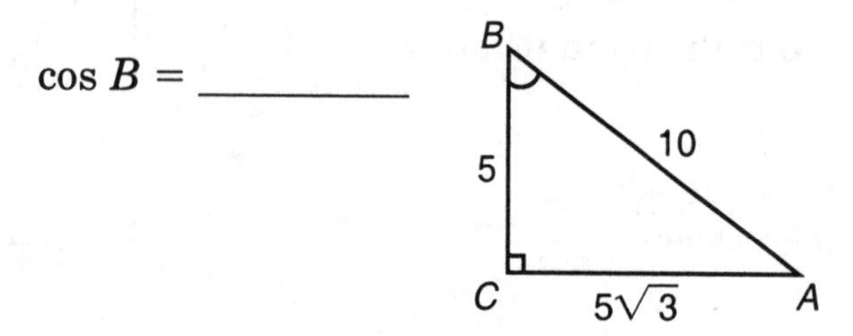

What does cos B reduce to as a fraction? ________________

Convert this reduced fraction to a decimal. Round to the nearest ten thousandth.

____

You also can use a table to find the sine, cosine, and tangent of acute angles.

Values of the Trigonometric Functions

Angle	Sin	Cos	Tan	Angle	Sin	Cos	Tan
1°	0.0175	0.9998	0.0175	46°	0.7193	0.6947	1.0355
2°	0.0349	0.9994	0.0349	47°	0.7314	0.6820	1.0724
3°	0.0523	0.9986	0.0524	48°	0.7431	0.6691	1.1106
4°	0.0698	0.9976	0.0699	49°	0.7547	0.6561	1.1504
5°	0.0872	0.9962	0.0875	50°	0.7660	0.6428	1.1918
6°	0.1045	0.9945	0.1054	51°	0.7771	0.6293	1.2349
7°	0.1219	0.9925	0.1228	52°	0.7880	0.6157	1.2799
8°	0.1392	0.9903	0.1405	53°	0.7986	0.6018	1.3270
9°	0.1564	0.9877	0.1584	54°	0.8090	0.5878	1.3764
10°	0.1736	0.9848	0.1763	55°	0.8192	0.5736	1.4281
11°	0.1908	0.9816	0.1944	56°	0.8290	0.5592	1.4826
12°	0.2079	0.9781	0.2126	57°	0.8387	0.5446	1.5399
13°	0.2250	0.9744	0.2309	58°	0.8480	0.5299	1.6003
14°	0.2419	0.9703	0.2493	59°	0.8572	0.5150	1.6643
15°	0.2588	0.9659	0.2679	60°	0.8660	0.5000	1.7321
16°	0.2756	0.9613	0.2867	61°	0.8746	0.4848	1.8040
17°	0.2924	0.9563	0.3057	62°	0.8829	0.4695	1.8807
18°	0.3090	0.9511	0.3249	63°	0.8910	0.4540	1.9626
19°	0.3256	0.9455	0.3443	64°	0.8988	0.4384	2.0503
20°	0.3420	0.9397	0.3640	65°	0.9063	0.4226	2.1445
21°	0.3584	0.9336	0.3839	66°	0.9135	0.4067	2.2460
22°	0.3746	0.9272	0.4040	67°	0.9205	0.3907	2.3559
23°	0.3907	0.9205	0.4245	68°	0.9272	0.3746	2.4751
24°	0.4067	0.9135	0.4452	69°	0.9336	0.3584	2.6051
25°	0.4226	0.9063	0.4663	70°	0.9397	0.3420	2.7475
26°	0.4384	0.8988	0.4877	71°	0.9455	0.3256	2.9042
27°	0.4540	0.8910	0.5095	72°	0.9511	0.3090	3.0777
28°	0.4695	0.8829	0.5317	73°	0.9563	0.2924	3.2709
29°	0.4848	0.8746	0.5543	74°	0.9613	0.2756	3.4874
30°	0.5000	0.8660	0.5774	75°	0.9659	0.2588	3.7321
31°	0.5150	0.8572	0.6009	76°	0.9703	0.2419	4.0108
32°	0.5299	0.8480	0.6249	77°	0.9744	0.2250	4.3315
33°	0.5446	0.8387	0.6494	78°	0.9781	0.2079	4.7046
34°	0.5592	0.8290	0.6745	79°	0.9816	0.1908	5.1446
35°	0.5736	0.8192	0.7002	80°	0.9848	0.1736	5.6713
36°	0.5878	0.8090	0.7265	81°	0.9877	0.1564	6.3138
37°	0.6018	0.7986	0.7536	82°	0.9903	0.1392	7.1154
38°	0.6157	0.7880	0.7813	83°	0.9925	0.1219	8.1443
39°	0.6293	0.7771	0.8098	84°	0.9945	0.1045	9.5144
40°	0.6428	0.7660	0.8391	85°	0.9962	0.0872	11.4301
41°	0.6561	0.7547	0.8693	86°	0.9976	0.0698	14.3007
42°	0.6691	0.7431	0.9004	87°	0.9986	0.0523	19.0811
43°	0.6820	0.7314	0.9325	88°	0.9994	0.0349	28.6363
44°	0.6947	0.7193	0.9657	89°	0.9998	0.0175	57.2900
45°	0.7071	0.7071	1.0000	90°	1.0000	0.0000	—

Example

If you know the measure of $\angle B = 60°$, you can find the sin B, cos B, and tan B in the right triangle shown by using the table.

$\sin B = 0.8660$

$\cos B = 0.5000$

$\tan B = 1.7321$

Practice

Directions: In Numbers 1 and 2, find the numerical values of the ratios. Use the table on page 79 to find the nearest whole degree measure of $\angle B$.

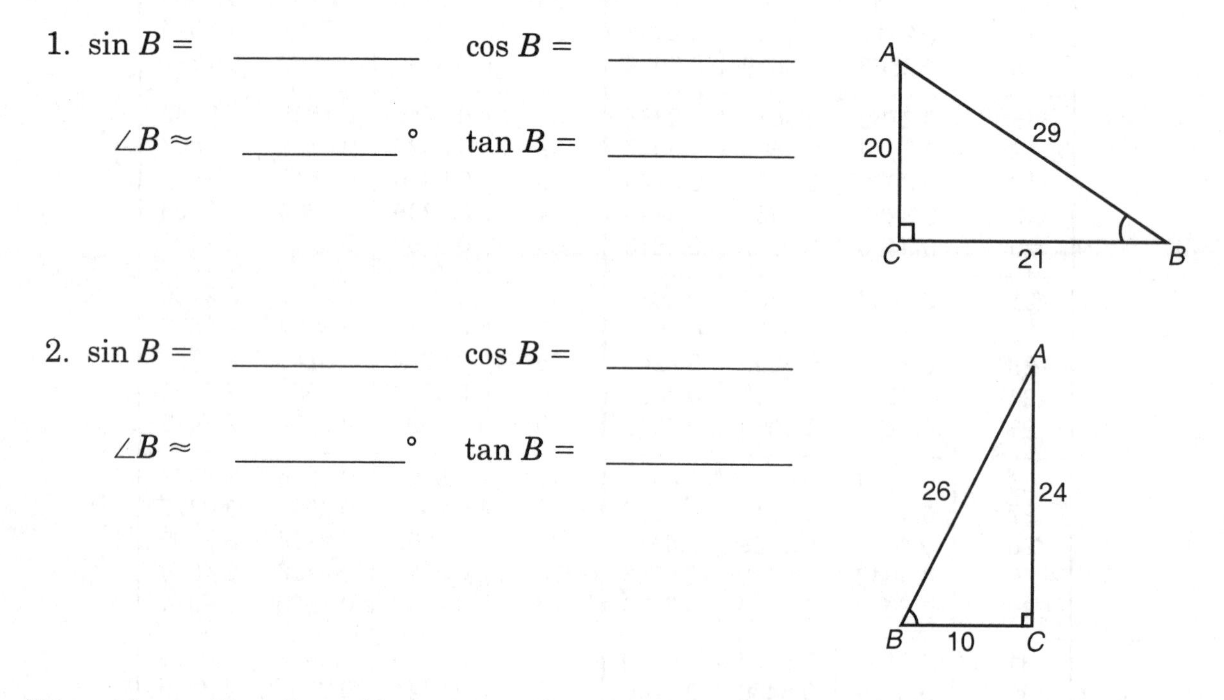

1. $\sin B =$ ________ $\cos B =$ ________

   $\angle B \approx$ ________° $\tan B =$ ________

2. $\sin B =$ ________ $\cos B =$ ________

   $\angle B \approx$ ________° $\tan B =$ ________

Directions: Use the table on page 79 to answer Numbers 3 through 6.

3. $\sin 45° =$ ________ $\cos 45° =$ ________ $\tan 45° =$ ________

4. $\sin 78° =$ ________ $\cos 78° =$ ________ $\tan 78° =$ ________

5. $\sin 7° =$ ________ $\cos 7° =$ ________ $\tan 7° =$ ________

6. $\sin 54° =$ ________ $\cos 54° =$ ________ $\tan 54° =$ ________

1. At Terrific Tacos, a certain task is supposed to take workers between 1 minute and 1.5 minutes. Which inequality expresses this range? Use n to represent time.

   A. $1 \geq n \geq 1.5$
   B. $1 \leq n \leq 1.5$
   C. $1.5 \leq n \leq 1$
   D. $1.5 \leq n \geq 1$

2. Tom bought several tickets to the rodeo for his family. Tickets were $6.25 each. Tom gave the cashier a $50 bill and received $18.75 in change. Which equation shows how many tickets (n) he bought?

   A. $\frac{50}{6.25} - 18.75 = n$
   B. $(6.25)n - 18.75 = 50$
   C. $(n + 18.75)(6.25) = 50$
   D. $6.25n = 50 - 18.75$

3. What is the value of $f(x) = 3x + 2$ when $x = 5$?

   ____

4. Triangle ABC is a right triangle.

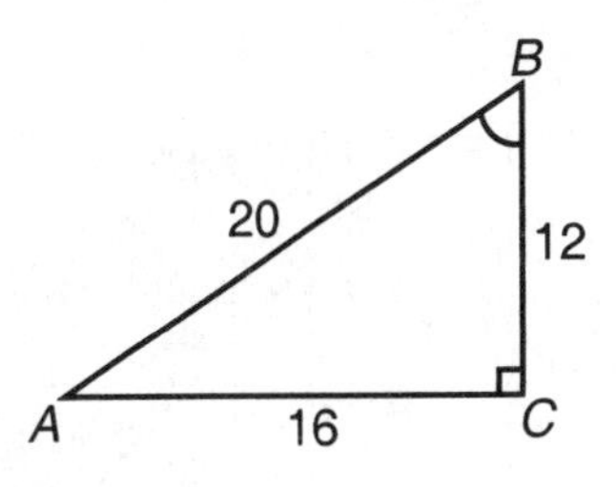

   What are the numerical values of the sine, cosine, and tangent of angle B?

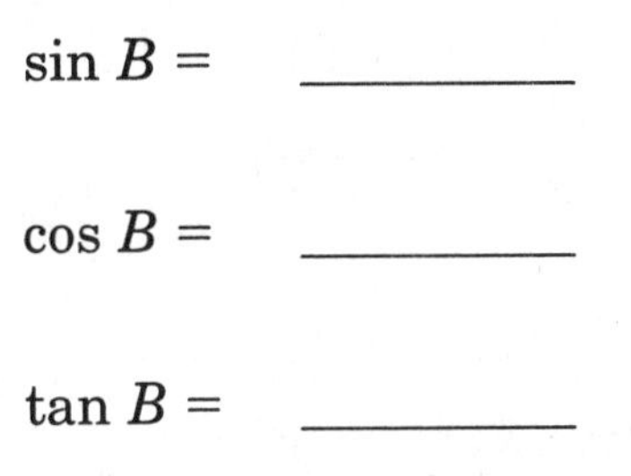

   $\sin B =$ __________

   $\cos B =$ __________

   $\tan B =$ __________

   What is the degree measure of angle B? (Round to the nearest degree.)

   $\angle B =$ __________ °

5. Which of the following sets of ordered pairs is a function?

   A. (5, 1), (5, 2), (5, 3)
   B. (3, 8), (4, 8), (5, 8)
   C. (8, 1), (4, 6), (4, 8)
   D. (5, 7), (5, 8), (6, 9)

6. Which is the solution to the system below?

$x + y \leq 5$

$2y \geq x - 2$

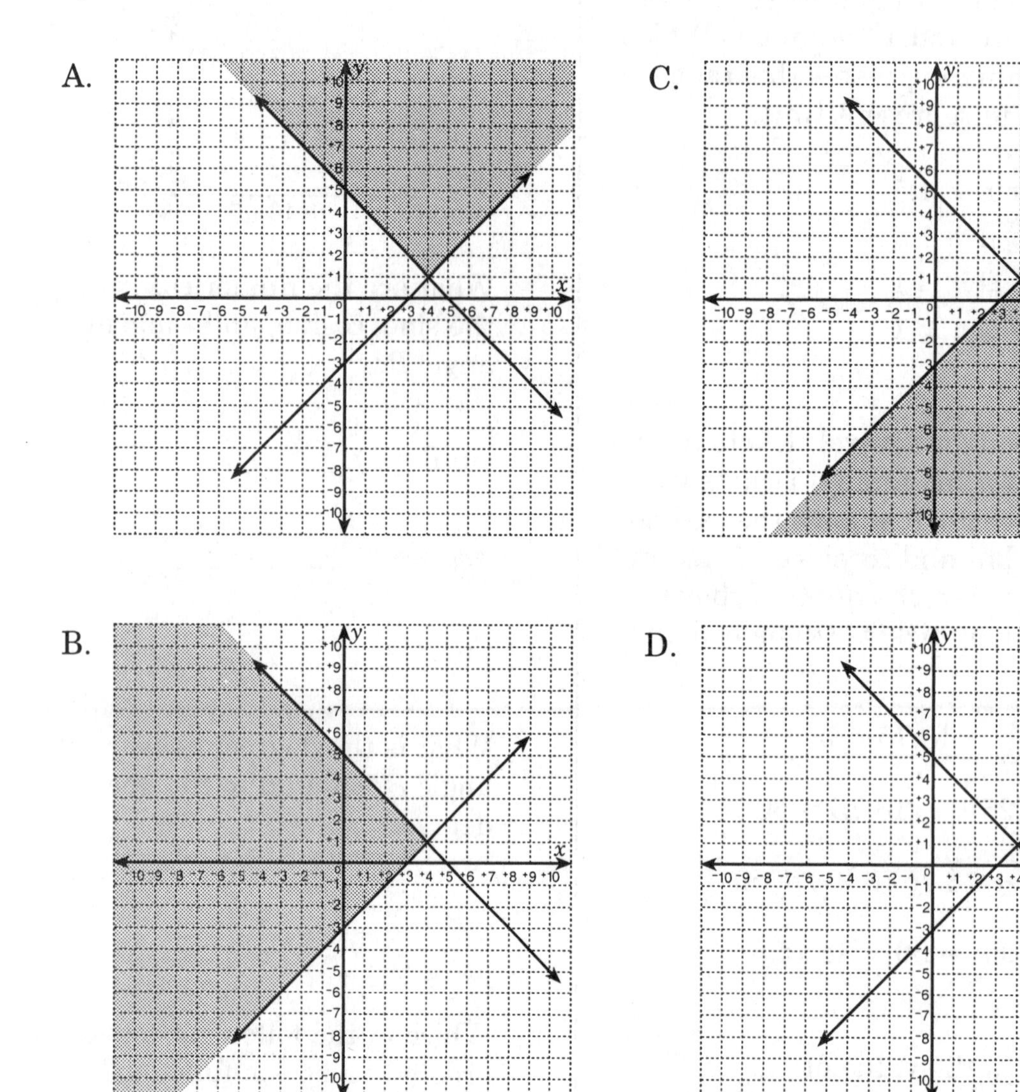

7. A 20-foot wire is stretched from the ground and attached close to the top of an antenna tower. The total height of the tower is 4 feet greater than the distance from the tower's base to the end of the wire.

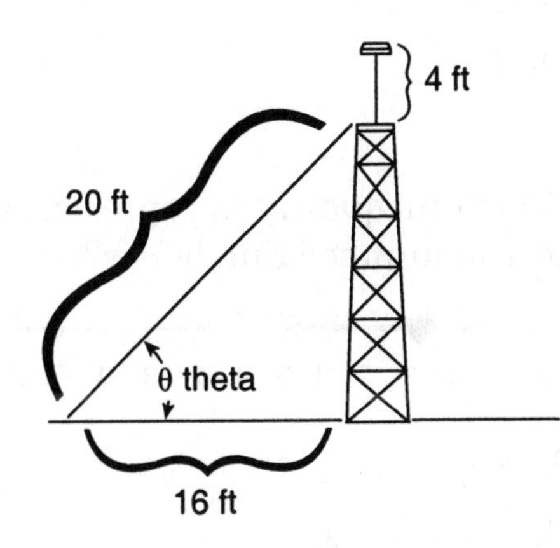

A. Find the total height of the tower.

____

B. Write an equation to calculate the angle of incline, marked as theta (θ) in the diagram.

____

C. To the nearest degree, what is the angle of incline? Show your work and explain your reasoning.

____

____

8. A size-6 dress in the United States corresponds to a size-36 dress in Italy. The following function will convert a United States dress size into an Italian dress size.

$f(x) = 2(x + 12)$

Which of the following Italian dress sizes corresponds to a size 10 in the United States?

A. 20
B. 22
C. 32
D. 44

9. Find the solutions for the quadratic equation

$2x^2 - 3x - 20 = 0$

Explain which method you used to find the solutions and show your work.

10. Solve the equation $2a + 3b = 6$ for the variable b.

____

11. Which of the following relations is also a function?

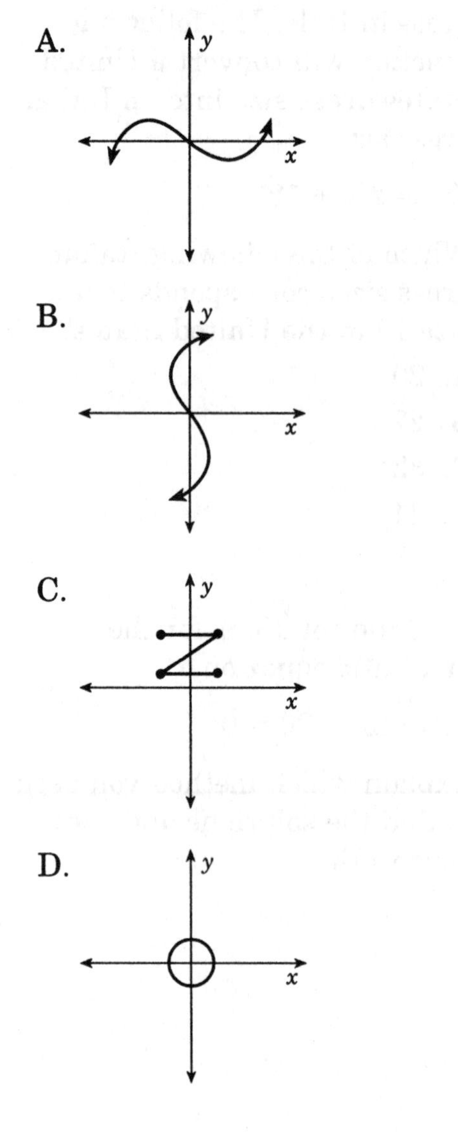

12. Write a matrix to represent this system of equations.

$x + 3y = 8$

$2x - 5y = 13$

13. What is the next number in this pattern?

10, 12, 11, 13, 12, 14

A. 10
B. 12
C. 13
D. 16

14. Which inequality is represented by the number line below?

$^-6\ ^-5\ ^-4\ ^-3\ ^-2\ ^-1\ 0\ 1\ 2\ 3\ 4\ 5\ 6$

A. $x < 0$

B. $^-3 < 0 \leq x$

C. $0 > x \geq\ ^-3$

D. $0 \geq x > 3$

15. In 1992, the population of the United States was about 249 million. Using an exponential growth function, experts are predicting that the population in 2002 will be 272 million.

A. What is the percent of increase in population from 1992 to 2002? Round your answer to the nearest whole percent.

____

B. Assume that the population continues to increase at this same rate over the next 10-year period. Write an expression to calculate the population of the United States in 2012.

____

16. Find the value of x.

$$\frac{4}{9} = \frac{5x + 3x}{45}$$

A. 2.5
B. 5.6
C. 8
D. 72

17. Six times the sum of 8 and another number (x) equals 78. Which of the following equations could you use to find the missing number?

A. $(6 + 8)(6 + x) = 78$
B. $78 - 6x = 8$
C. $6(8 + x) = 78$
D. $6x + 8x = 78$

18. Gino saves $5.00 every week by putting the money into a piggy bank. He does this 52 weeks a year for 4 years. Which of the equations below would represent the total amount of money (s) Gino has saved?

A. $5 + 52 + 4 = s$
B. $5 \bullet 52 + 4 = s$
C. $5 + 52 \bullet 4 = s$
D. $5 \bullet 52 \bullet 4 = s$

19. Which of the following equations represents a quadratic function?

A. $x^2 - 6x + 10 = 5$
B. $x^2 + y^2 = 16$
C. $x - y = 4$
D. $x^3 = 8$

20. Which of the following ratios shows the cosine of an acute angle of a right triangle?

A. $\frac{\text{length of opposite side}}{\text{length of hypotenuse}}$

B. $\frac{\text{length of adjacent side}}{\text{length of hypotenuse}}$

C. $\frac{\text{length of adjacent side}}{\text{length of opposite side}}$

D. $\frac{\text{length of opposite side}}{\text{length of adjacent side}}$

Geometry and Measurement

Lesson 7: Geometry and Spatial Sense

Lesson 8: Measurement

Lesson 9: Geometry from an Algebraic Perspective

Lesson 7: Geometry and Spatial Sense

The word **geometry** literally means **earth measurement**.

Points, Lines, and Planes

Point: a single location, or position, having no size or dimension

Plane: a flat surface without thickness, extending in all directions

Line: all the points on a straight path that extends infinitely in both directions

Ray: all the points on a straight path that extends infinitely in one direction from an endpoint

Line segment: all the points on the straight path between two points, including those two points called endpoints

Intersecting lines: lines that meet at a point

Parallel lines: lines in the same plane that never intersect

Perpendicular lines: lines that meet to form right angles (right angles = 90°)

Perpendicular bisector: line, ray, or segment which divides a line segment into two equal parts

Transversal: a line that intersects two or more lines in the same plane at different points

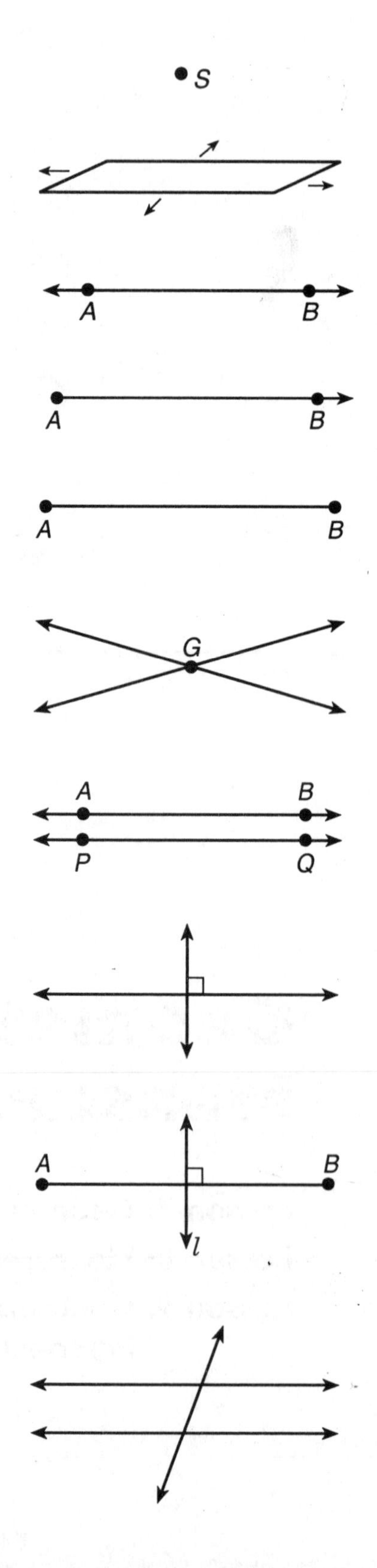

Angles

An **angle** is formed by two rays that share the same endpoint. The shared point is called the **vertex**. The rays are called **sides**.

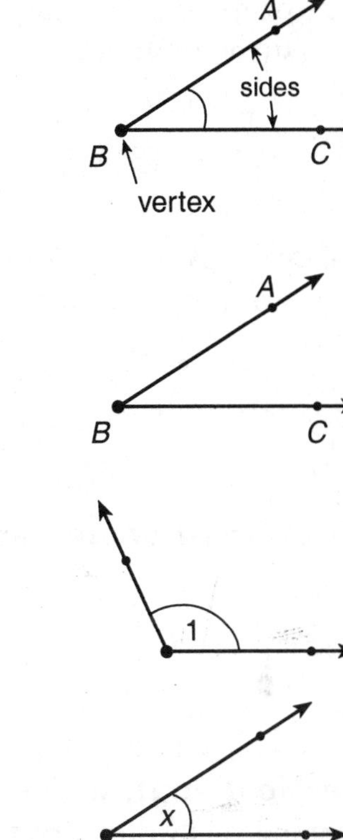

Angles can be named in different ways:

- by the letter of the vertex or by the letters of the three points that form it

  $\angle B$, $\angle ABC$, or $\angle CBA$

  (The letter in the center names the vertex.)

- by the number or small letter in its interior

  $\angle 1$ $\angle x$

Special angles

Right angle: has a measure of 90°

Measure (m) $\angle XYZ = 90°$

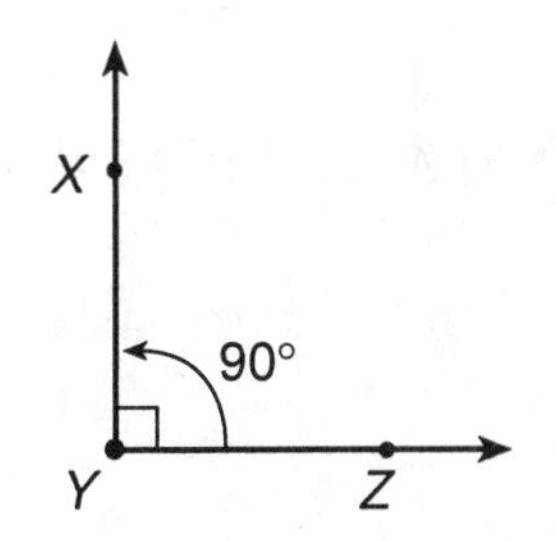

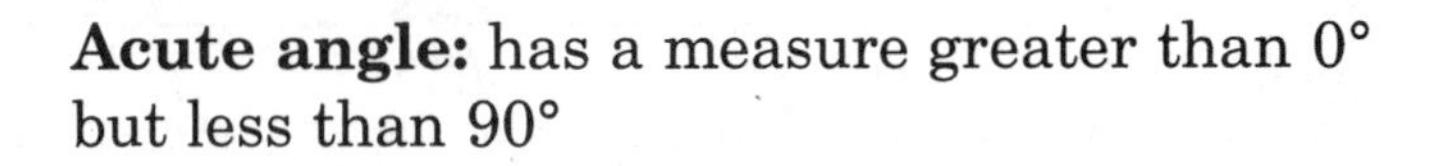

Acute angle: has a measure greater than 0° but less than 90°

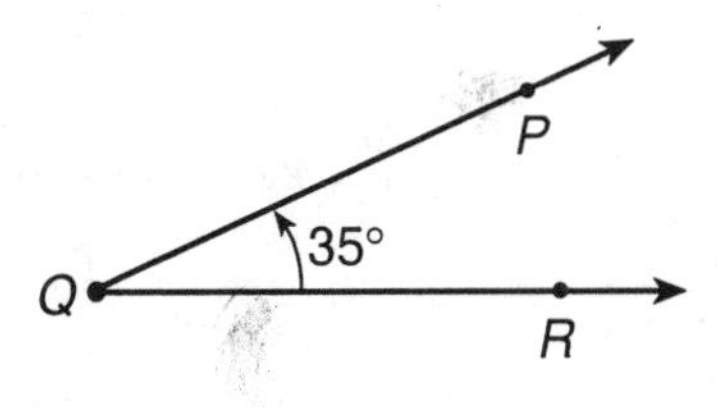

Obtuse angle: has a measure greater than 90° but less than 180°

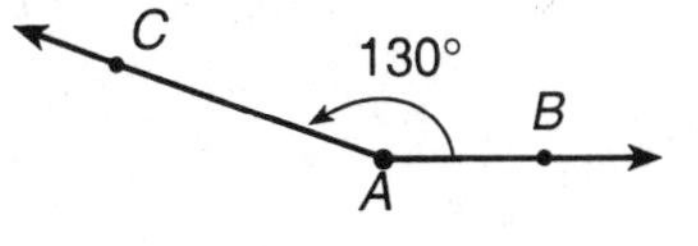

Straight angle: has a measure of 180°; its sides form a straight line

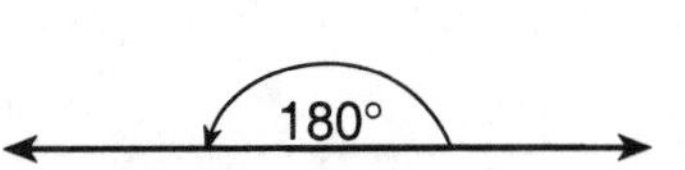

Supplementary angles: two angles whose measures have a sum of 180°

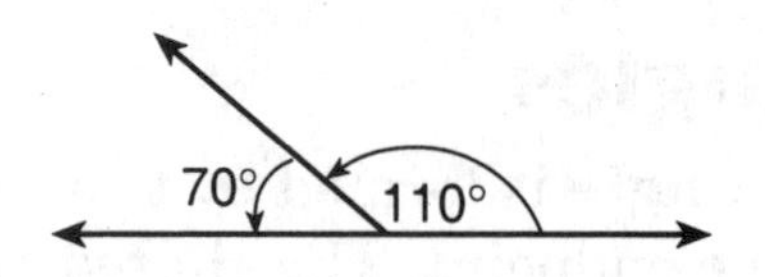

Complementary angles: two angles whose measures have a sum of 90°

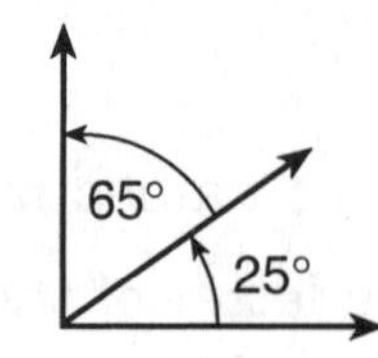

Congruent angles: angles that have the same measure

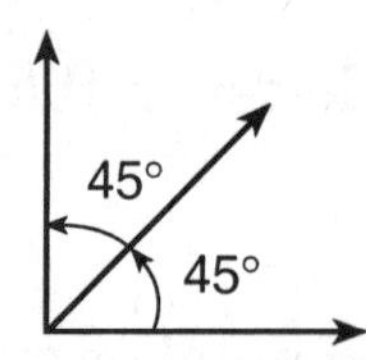

Vertical angles: pairs of congruent angles formed by two intersecting lines

$\angle 1 \cong \angle 3$

$\angle 2 \cong \angle 4$

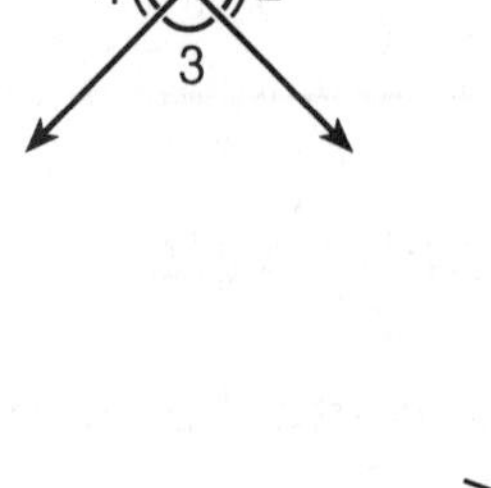

More special angles

$\angle 1$ and $\angle 2$ are **alternate interior** angles.

$\angle 1 \cong \angle 2$

$\angle 3$ and $\angle 4$ are **alternate exterior** angles.

$\angle 3 \cong \angle 4$

$\angle 3$ and $\angle 5$ are **corresponding** angles.

$\angle 3 \cong \angle 5$

$\angle 5$ and $\angle 2$ are **supplementary** angles.

$m\,\angle 5 + m\,\angle 2 = 180°$

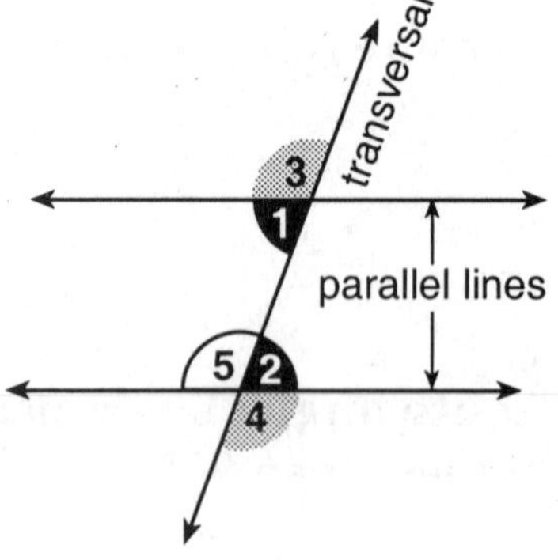

1. Use the two figures below to answer the following.

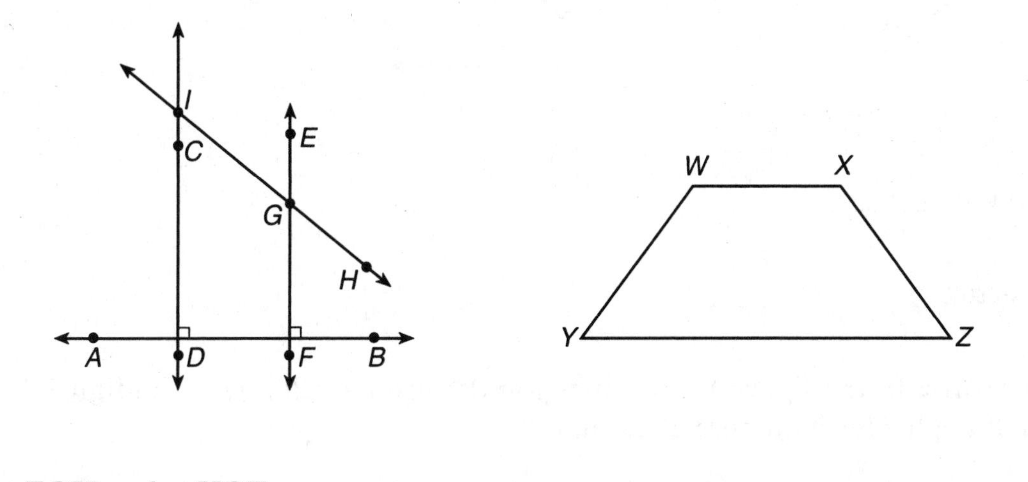

$\angle EGH$ and $\angle HGF$ are ______________

$\overleftrightarrow{AB}$ is a ______________

$\overline{WY}$ is a ______________

$\overrightarrow{GH}$ is a ______________

Name a pair of parallel lines: ______________________________________

Name a transversal line: ______________________________________

$\overleftrightarrow{AB}$ and $\overleftrightarrow{CD}$ are ______________________________________ lines

2. What type of angle is each of the following?

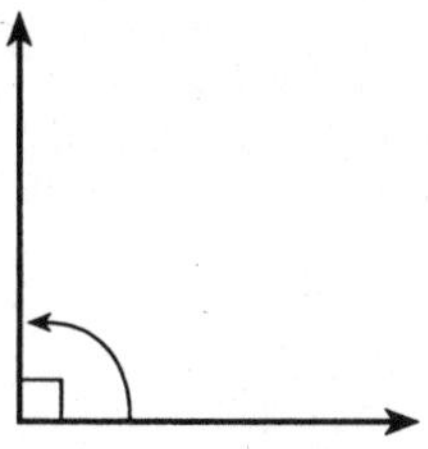

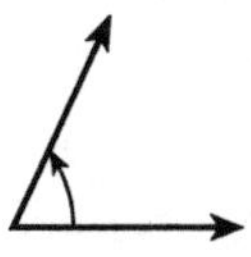

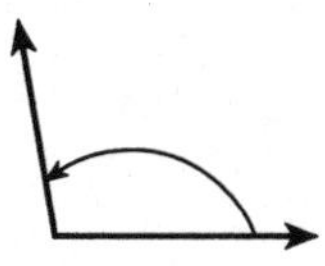

______________ ______________ ______________

3. Name the angle and vertex in this figure.

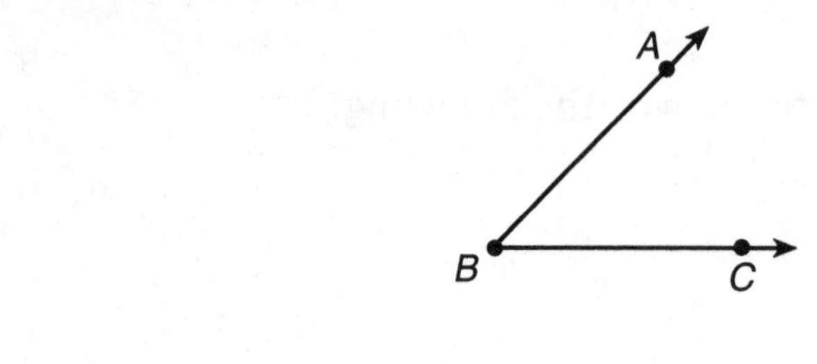

angle ______________

vertex ______________

Directions: In the figure below, lines *j* and *k* are parallel. Use the figure to list pairs of angles for Numbers 4 through 7.

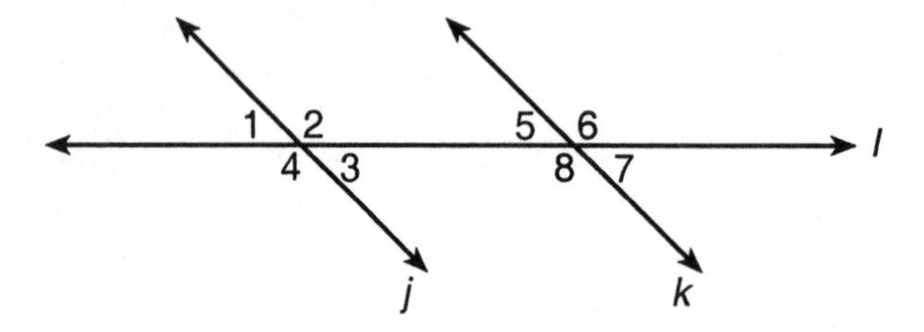

4. corresponding angles ______________________________

5. supplementary angles ______________________________

6. alternate interior angles ______________________________

7. alternate exterior angles ______________________________

Two-Dimensional Figures

Two-dimensional figures lie on a plane. Their two dimensions are length and width. Polygons are examples of two-dimensional figures.

Quadrilaterals

A **polygon** that has 4 sides is called a **quadrilateral**.

Quadrilaterals: Polygons with 4 Sides

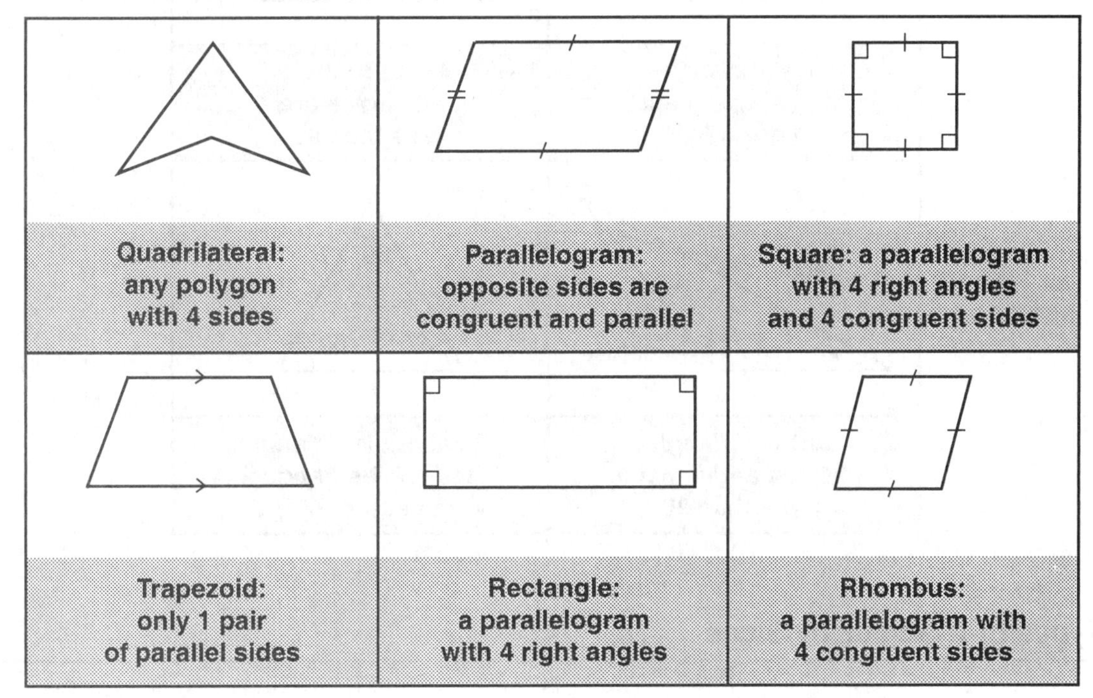

Quadrilateral: any polygon with 4 sides
Parallelogram: opposite sides are congruent and parallel
Square: a parallelogram with 4 right angles and 4 congruent sides
Trapezoid: only 1 pair of parallel sides
Rectangle: a parallelogram with 4 right angles
Rhombus: a parallelogram with 4 congruent sides

Other Common Polygons

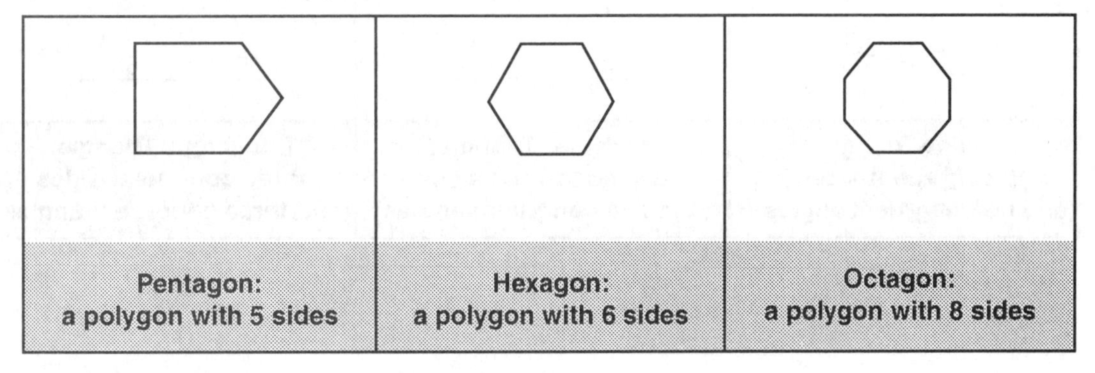

Pentagon: a polygon with 5 sides
Hexagon: a polygon with 6 sides
Octagon: a polygon with 8 sides

A **regular polygon** is a polygon in which all sides and all angles are congruent.

Triangles

Triangles are named by the characteristics of their sides and angles.

Types of Triangles by Angles

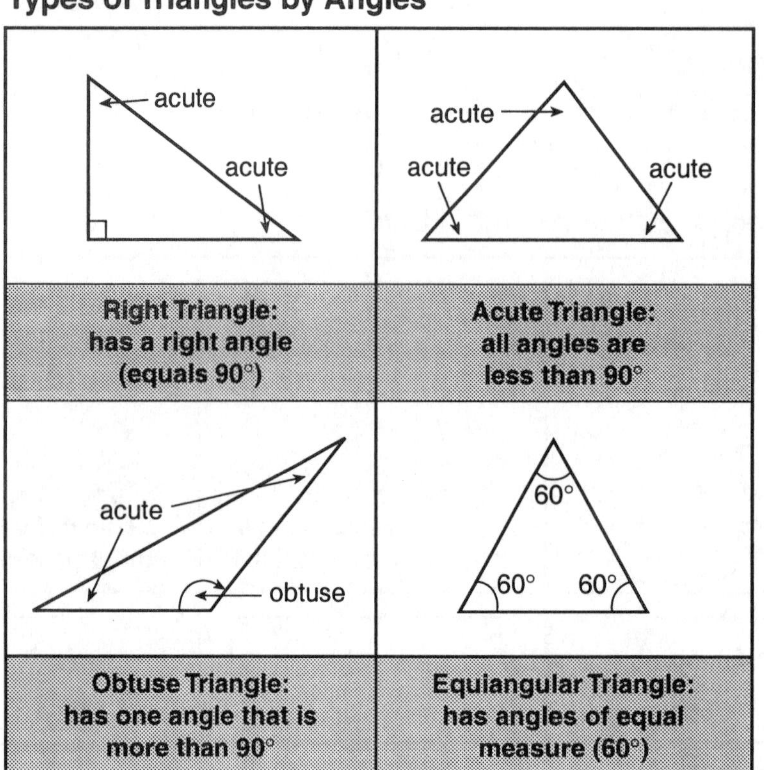

Types of Triangles by Sides

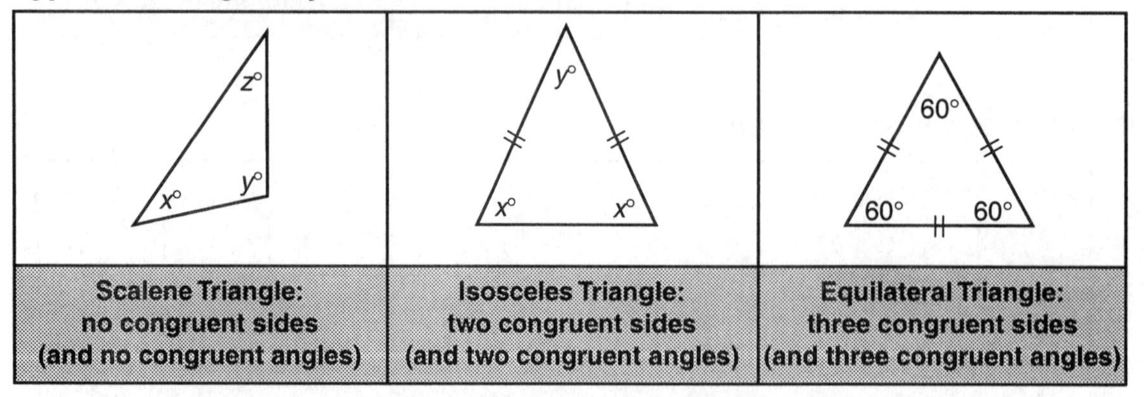

The sum of the measures of the interior angles of a triangle is 180°.

The Pythagorean Theorem

The **Pythagorean Theorem** says that for any right triangle, the square of the length of the hypotenuse is equal to the sum of the squares of the lengths of the other two sides.

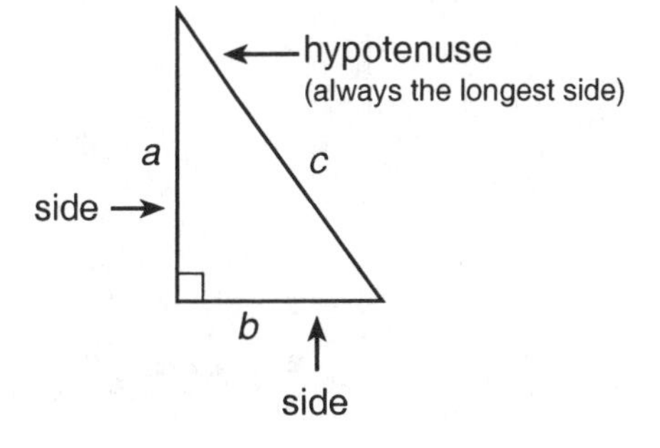

This information can be expressed with the equation:

$$a^2 + b^2 = c^2$$

A theorem is a statement that can be proven. The diagram below gives us visual proof of the Pythagorean Theorem.

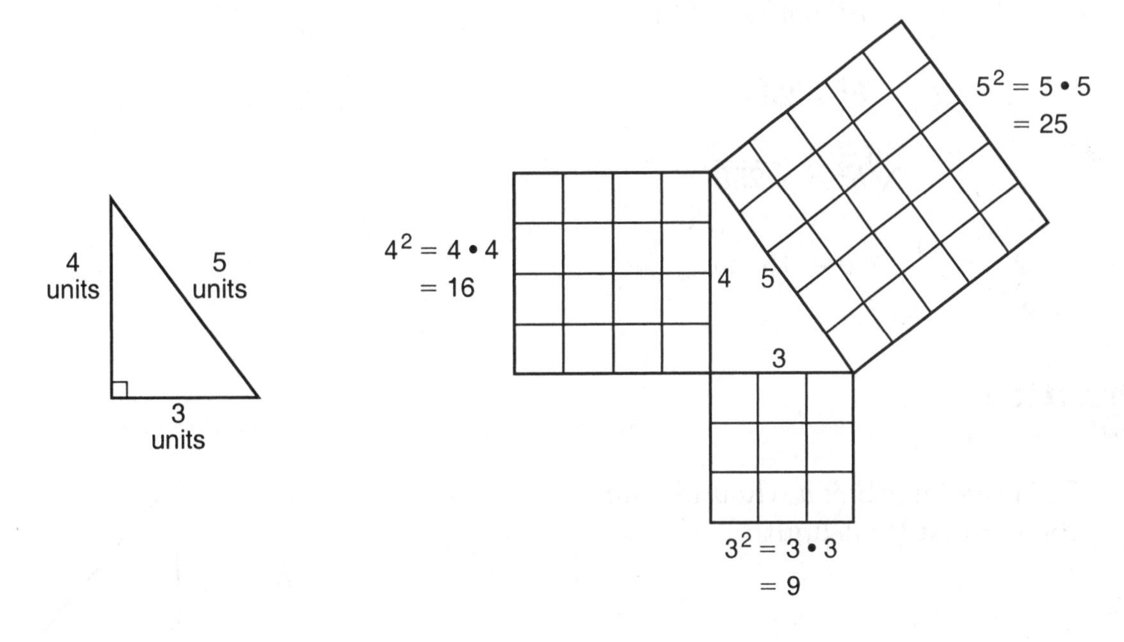

The units that represent the squares of sides a and b add up to the units that represent the square of the hypotenuse, or side c.

If you know the lengths of any two sides of a right triangle, and you know which side is the hypotenuse, you can find the length of the third side.

Example

Look at the figure below. What is the length of b?

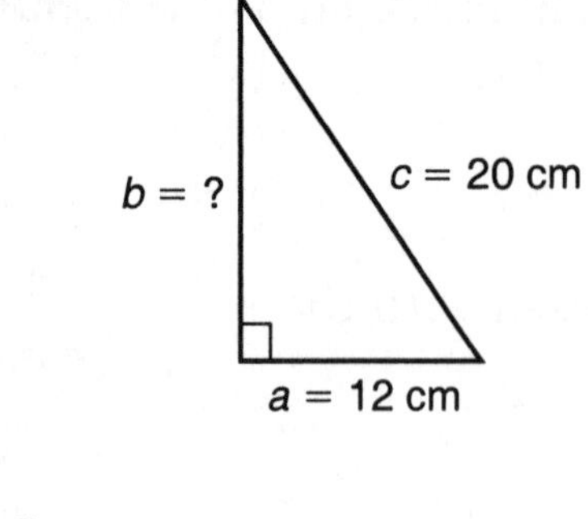

$$\boldsymbol{a^2 + b^2 = c^2}$$

$$12^2 + b^2 = 20^2$$

$$144 + b^2 = 400$$

$$b^2 = 400 - 144$$

$$b^2 = 256$$

$$\sqrt{b^2} = \sqrt{256}$$

$$b = 16 \text{ cm}$$

Practice

1. Find the length of a. (Round your answer to the nearest thousandth.)

   ____

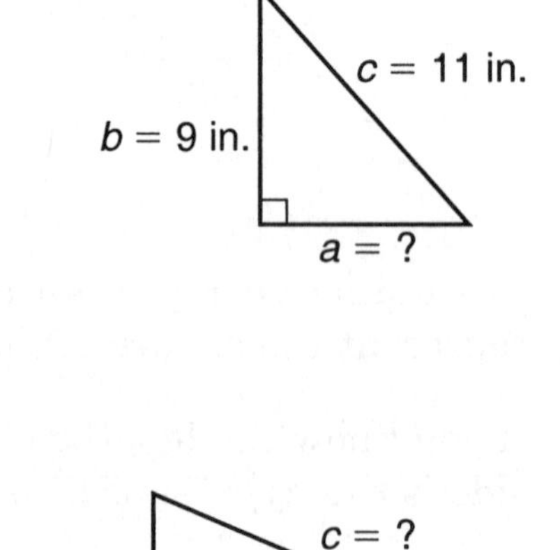

2. Find the length of c. _______________

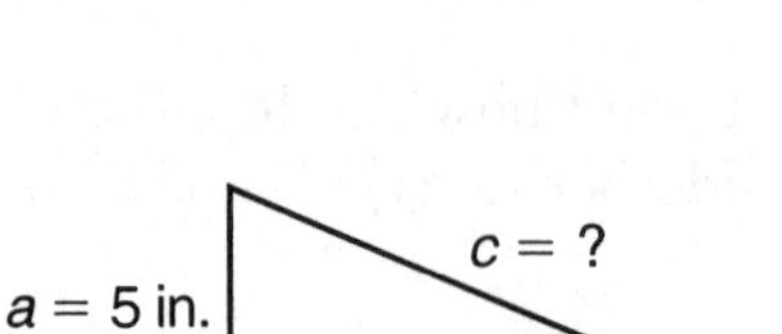

Special Right Triangles

(45°–45°–90°) right triangle

An isosceles right triangle with two acute angles of 45°.

The sides opposite the 45° angles are congruent, and the hypotenuse is $\sqrt{2}$ times larger.

The ratio of the sides is $x : x : x\sqrt{2}$

(30°–60°–90°) right triangle

A right triangle with two acute angles of 30° and 60°.

The side opposite the 60° angle is $\sqrt{3}$ times the size of the side opposite the 30° angle; the hypotenuse is 2 times the size of the side opposite the 30° angle.

The ratio of the sides is $x : x\sqrt{3} : 2x$

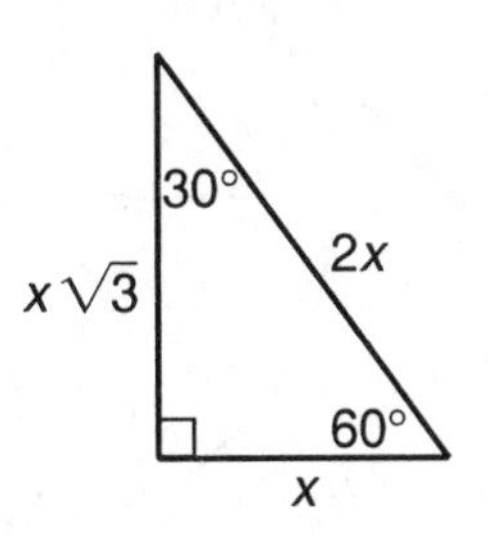

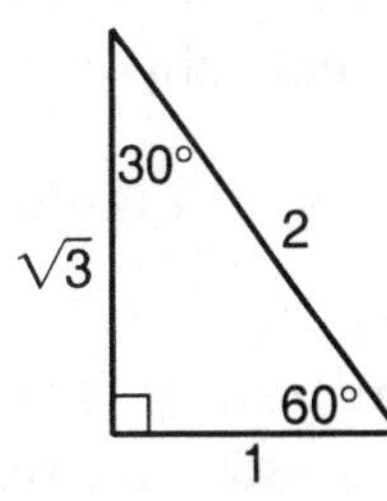

Circles

A **circle** consists of all points in a plane that are an equal distance from a given point, called the center. The center point names the circle.

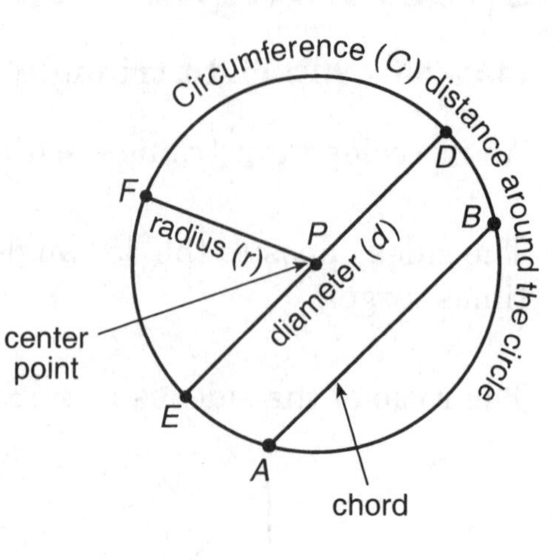

Radius (*r*): a line segment from the center point to any point on the circle. All radii (plural of radius) are equal in length.

Diameter (*d*): a line segment that passes through the center and has both endpoints on the circle. All diameters are equal in length.

Chord: a line segment that has both endpoints lying on the circle

Arc: a portion of a circle that includes two endpoints and all the points in between

Circumference (*C*): the distance around the circle

Secant: any line, ray, or segment that contains a chord

$\overleftrightarrow{AB}$ is a secant in circle Y.

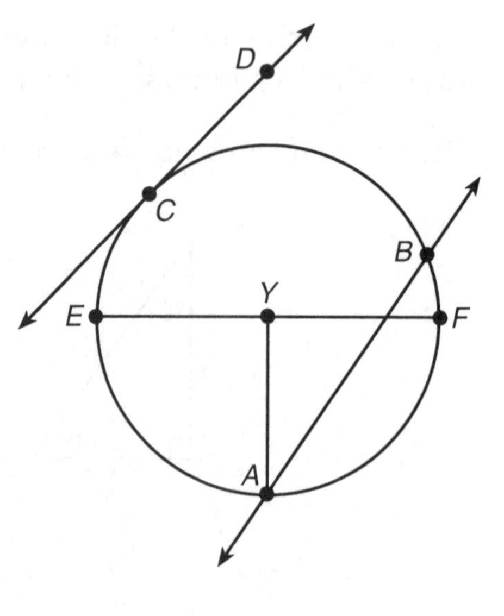

Tangent: any line, ray, or segment in the same plane that intersects the circle at one point

$\overleftrightarrow{DC}$ is a tangent in circle Y.

The **point of tangency** is the point where a tangent line intercepts a circle. A circle has an infinite number of points of tangency.

C is the point of tangency for $\overleftrightarrow{DC}$ on circle Y.

Practice

Directions: Use the circle below to label parts given in Numbers 1 through 6.

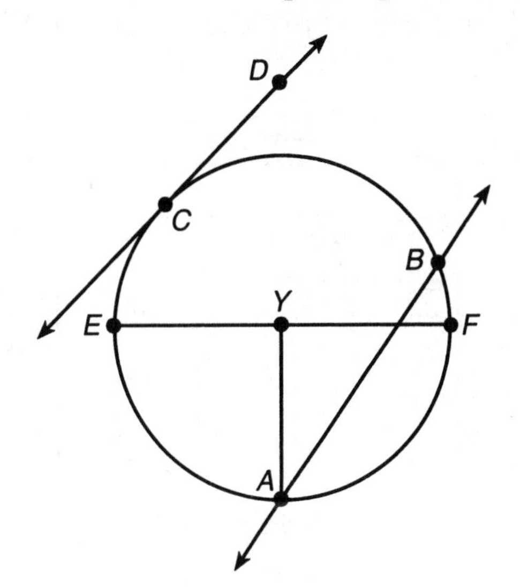

1. $\overset{\frown}{CB}$ ____________________

2. Y ____________________

3. $\overline{EF}$ ____________________

4. $\overline{YA}$ ____________________

5. $\overline{AB}$ ____________________

6. $\overleftrightarrow{AB}$ ____________________

7. Explain why a diameter is always a chord, but a chord is not always a diameter.

____

____

____

Three-Dimensional Figures

Solid figures are three-dimensional. Their dimensions are length, width, and height. The flat surfaces of a three-dimensional figure are called **faces**. The sides are called **edges**. The point where the edges meet is the **vertex**.

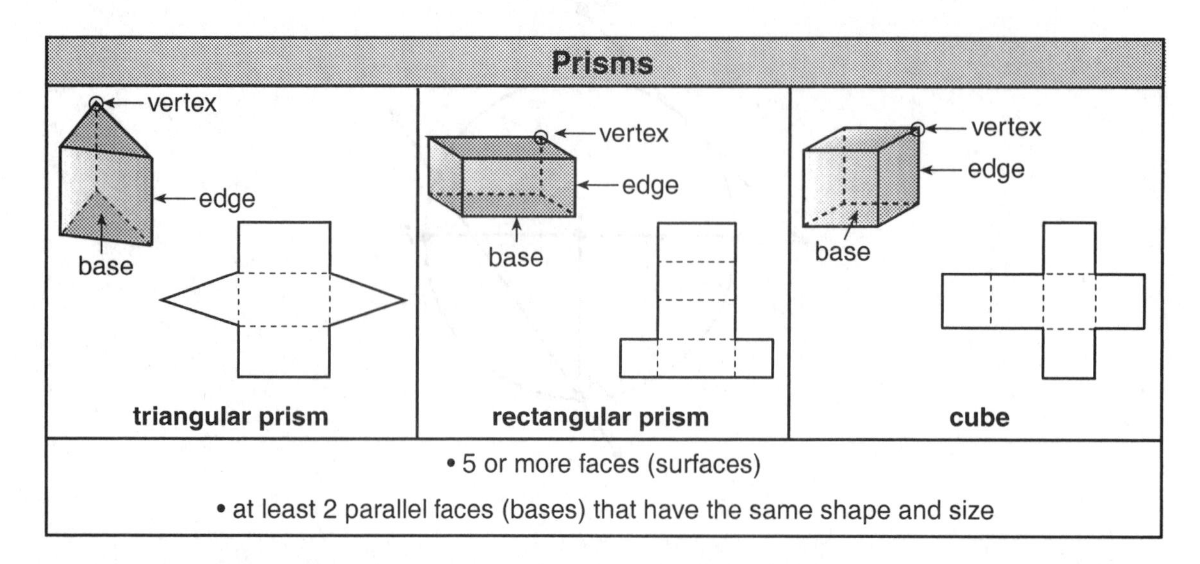

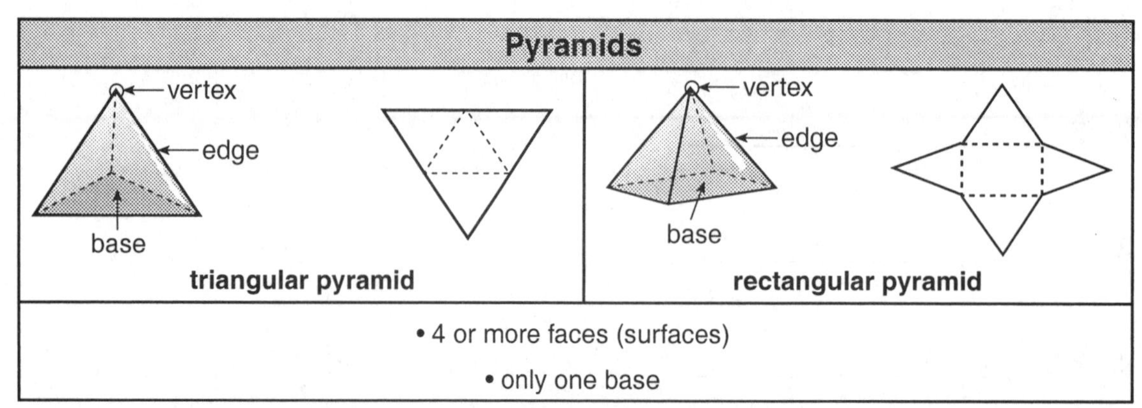

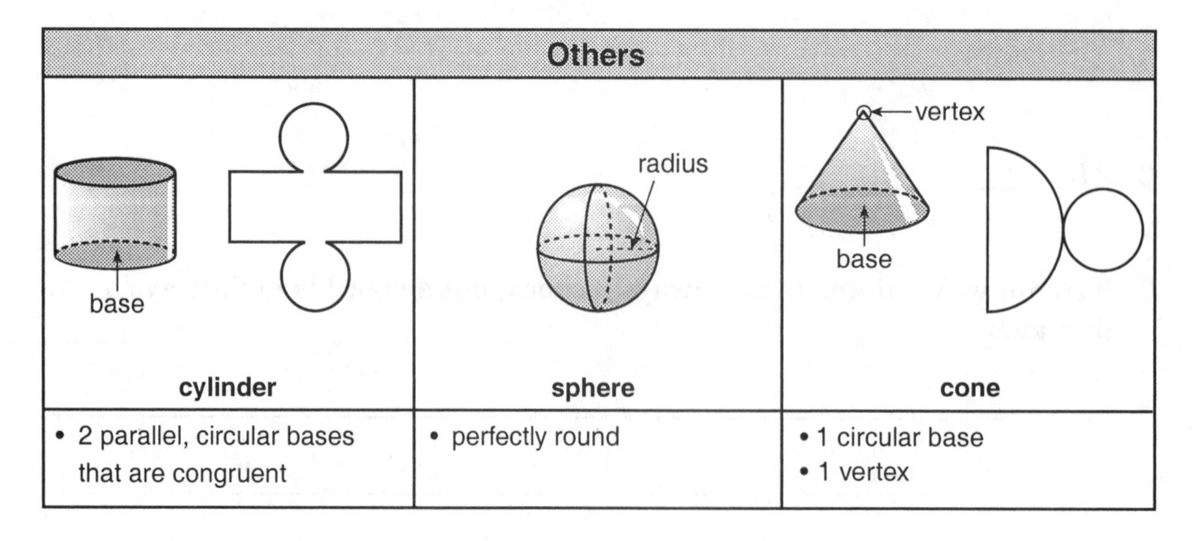

Others
base
cylinder
radius
sphere
vertex
base
cone
• 2 parallel, circular bases that are congruent
• perfectly round
• 1 circular base
• 1 vertex

Views of 3-dimensional figures

The drawings below show 3 views of the figure on the right.

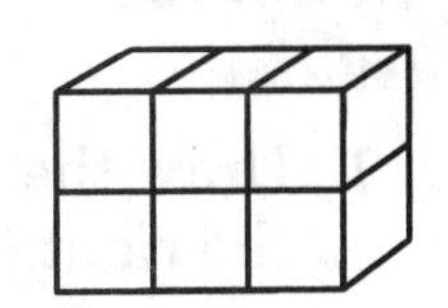

This is the front or back view.

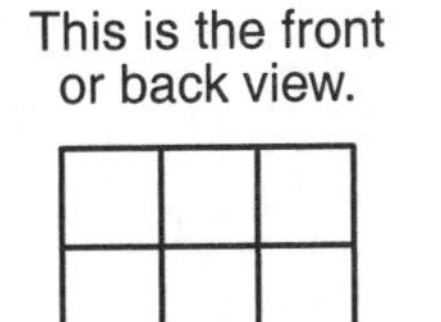

This is the top or bottom view.

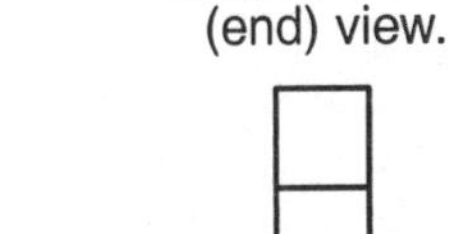

This is a side (end) view.

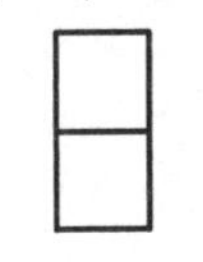

Example

The drawings below represent different views of the arrangement of cubes on the right.

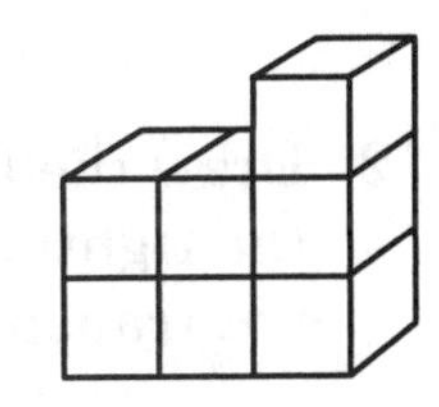

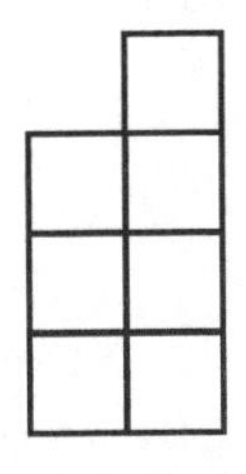

not a possible view

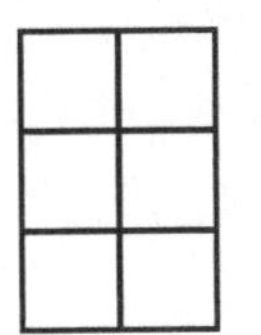

not a possible view

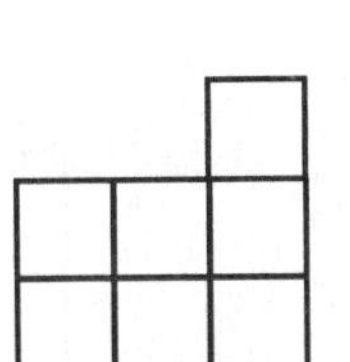

front view

top or bottom view

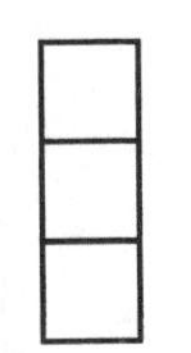

side (end) view

1. Draw the following views of the arrangement of cubes to the right: top, front, back, side, and bottom. Label each view.

2. Draw the following views of the triangular-based pyramid to the right: top, front, and bottom. (Assume that the pyramid is not transparent.)

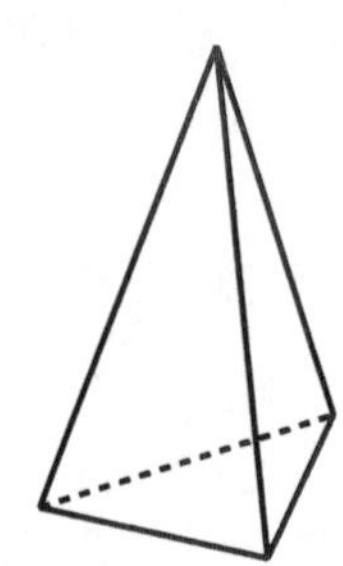

3. Draw the top view of the figure to the right.

4. Draw the top view of the figure to the right.

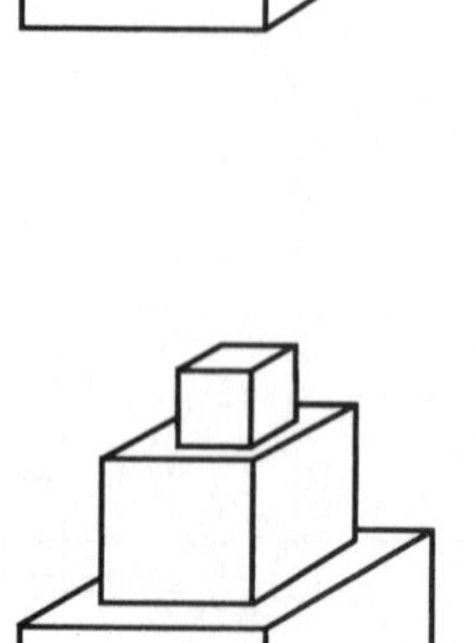

Planar cross-section

When a solid figure is cut by a plane, a plane figure is exposed. The plane figure is called a **planar cross-section**. A planar cross-section can be cut in any direction. The following examples show a solid being cut and the plane figure that is exposed.

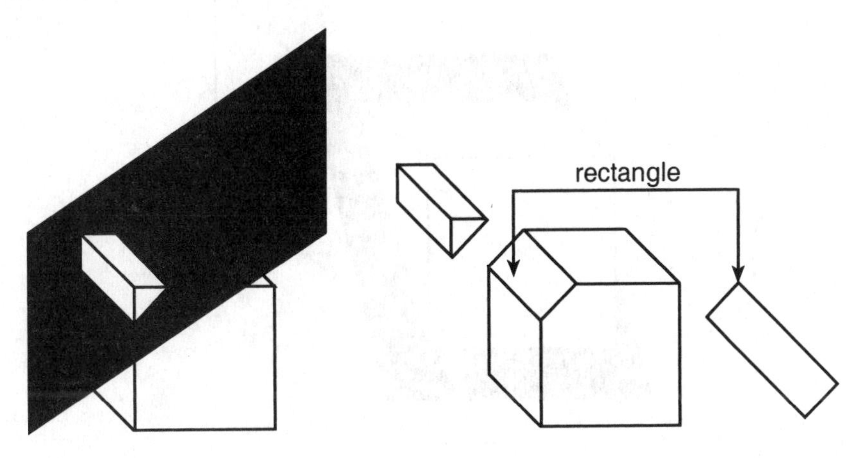

The cut produces a rectangular cross-section.

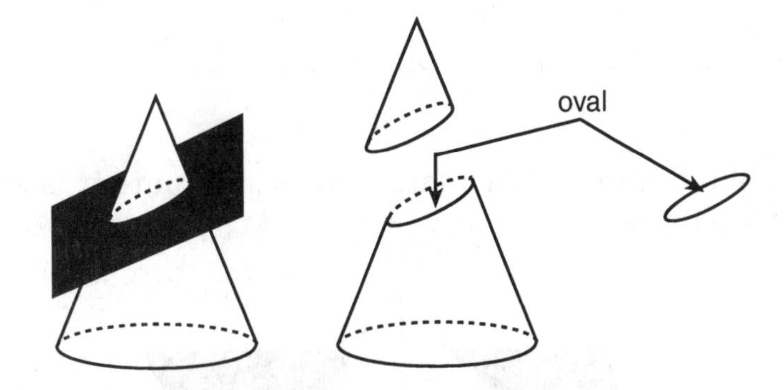

The cut produces an oval-shaped cross-section.

Cuts that are made parallel to the base(s) of a solid figure produce cross-sections called **right sections**.

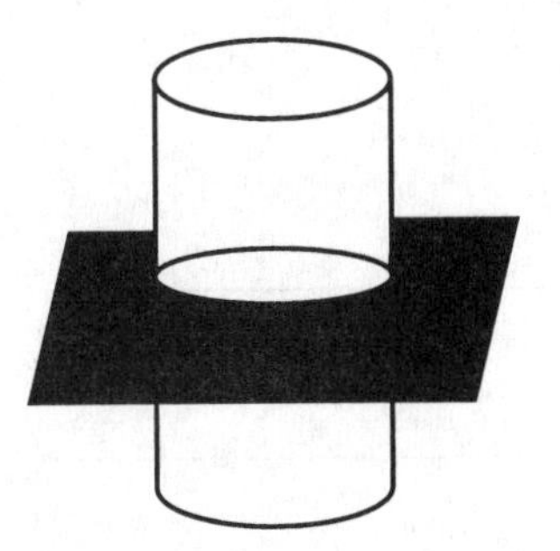

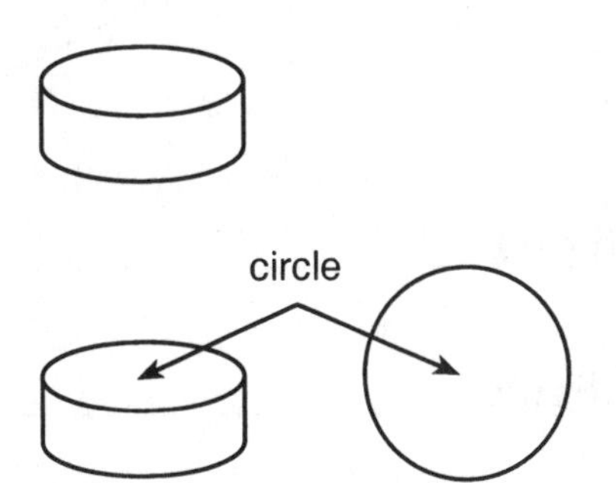

The cut produces a circular cross-section.

1. Identify the solid figure and its planar cross-section that is exposed when the solid is cut as shown.

solid figure: ______________________________

plane figure: ______________________________

2. Identify the solid figure and its planar cross-section that is exposed when the solid is cut as shown.

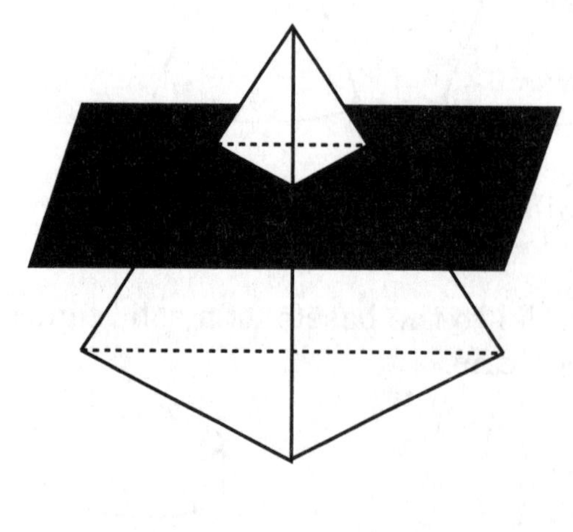

solid figure: ______________________________

plane figure: ______________________________

Special Investigation: Constructing Proofs

Mathematical assertions can be proved in many different ways. In a **direct proof**, you assume the conclusion is true and apply theorems, postulates, and definitions to prove that the conclusion must follow.

Example

Given: $\triangle ABC$; $\angle 3$ is supplementary to $\angle 4$

Prove: $m\angle 1 + m\angle 2 = m\angle 4$

B 2 A 1 3 4 C

Proof:

Statements	Reasons
1. $m\angle 1 + m\angle 2 + m\angle 3 = 180$	1. The sum of the measures of the interior angles of a triangle is 180°
2. $m\angle 3 + m\angle 4 = 180$	2. Definition of supplementary angles
3. $m\angle 1 + m\angle 2 + m\angle 3 = m\angle 3 + m\angle 4$	3. Substitution property
4. $m\angle 1 + m\angle 2 = m\angle 4$	4. Subtraction property

This proves that the measure of an exterior angle of a triangle equals the sum of the measures of the two remote interior angles.

In an **indirect** proof, you temporarily assume the conclusion is **not true** and use logic and reasoning to reach a **contradiction**. Once you reach a contradiction, you can state that the assumption must be false, and that the conclusion must then be true.

Example

Given: $m\angle A = 55°$, $m\angle B = 65°$

Prove: $\angle A$ and $\angle B$ are not vertical angles

Assume $\angle A$ and $\angle B$ **are** vertical angles. Then $m\angle A = m\angle B$ because vertical angles have equal measures. But this contradicts the fact that $m\angle A = 55°$ and $m\angle B = 65°$. Therefore, the temporary assumption that $\angle A$ and $\angle B$ are vertical angles must be false. It follows that $\angle A$ and $\angle B$ are not vertical angles.

Mathematical induction is a method of providing a hypothesis that is thought to be true for all counting numbers. This method involves a combination of inductive and deductive reasoning. Induction usually provides the conjecture, but it is deduction that proves it.

Example

Karl Friedrich Gauss was one of the most brilliant mathematicians of all time. When Gauss was very young, he was told by his school teacher to find the sum of the first 100 counting numbers. Gauss solved the problem in a matter of seconds by observing that there were 50 pairs of numbers that each added up to 101.

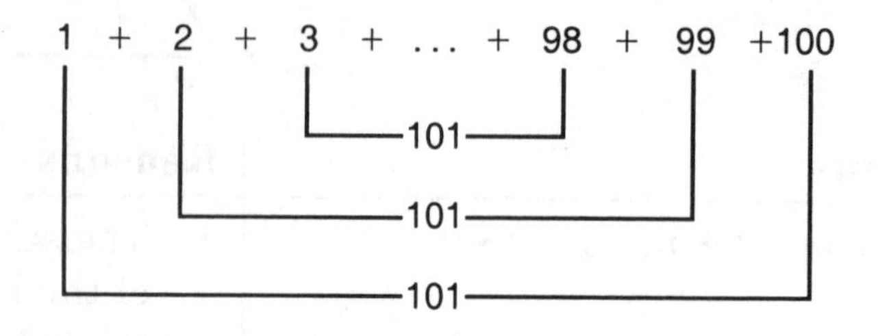

The sum of all the first 100 counting numbers is $50 \bullet 101 = 5{,}050$.

Example

Find the sum of the first 100 odd integers.

Rather than immediately computing the entire sum, look at the partial sums and notice the pattern:

$1 = 1$

$1 + 3 = 4$

$1 + 3 + 5 = 9$

$1 + 3 + 5 + 7 = 16$

.

.

.

The sums are the squares of consecutive positive integers starting with 1. It appears likely that the sum of the first 100 odd integers equals $100^2 = 10{,}000$. In general, we can hypothesize that the sum of the first n odd numbers is n^2.

Therefore, $1 + 3 + 5 + 7 + 9 + \ldots + 199 = 10{,}000$.

These exercises are designed to help you think through the steps needed to construct proofs.

Practice

1. Given: $\overline{GL} = \overline{AD}$

   Prove: $\overline{GA} = \overline{LD}$

   G L A D

   A. What segment is common to both $\overline{GA}$ and $\overline{LD}$? ____________

   B. Fill in the blanks. $\overline{GL}$ + _____ = $\overline{AD}$ + _____

   C. Fill in the blanks. $\overline{GL}$ + _____ = _____

   _____ + $\overline{AD}$ = _____

   D. Can you now say that $\overline{GA} = \overline{LD}$? ____________ If yes, by what property?

   (Hint: Look on page 105.) ____________

2. Provide a counterexample to show that each statement is false (use words or draw a picture).

   A. If $x^2 = 49$, then $x = 7$. ____________

   B. If $ab = 0$, then $a < 0$. ____________

   C. If a four-sided figure has four right angles, then it has four congruent sides.

   ____

3. A long time ago, a sorcerer presented a king with a small bottle. "This bottle," said he, "holds a liquid so powerful that it will instantly dissolve anything it touches." How did the king know the man was lying?

   ____

   ____

Lesson 8: Measurement

This lesson reviews how to solve different types of measurement problems.

Measures of the Interior Angles of a Polygon

The formula to find the sum of the measures of interior angles of a polygon is derived from dividing a polygon into a number of triangles. Choose a vertex of that polygon and draw all possible diagonals from that vertex.

Example

Find the sum of the measures of the interior angles of an octagon.

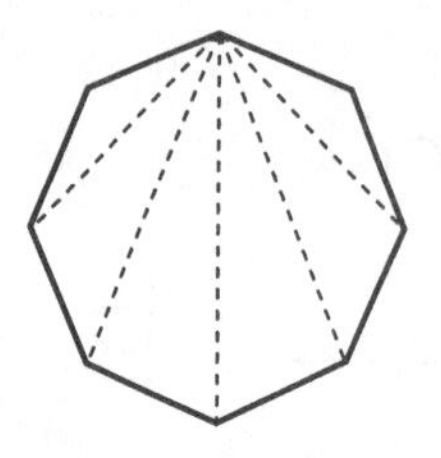

There are 6 triangles, and since there are 180° in each triangle, we multiply:

$6(180) = 1{,}080°$

The number of triangles that the octagon can be divided into is 2 less than the number of sides. We can extend this rule to say that if a polygon has n sides, then it can be divided into $n - 2$ triangles.

So, the sum of the measures of the interior angles of a polygon is **180 (n – 2)**.

To find the measure of one interior angle of a polygon, use

$$\frac{180(n-2)}{n}$$

Using the formula, we can find the measure of one interior angle of an octagon.

$$\frac{1{,}080}{8} = 135°$$

Perimeter

Perimeter is the distance around a polygon.

To find the perimeter of a polygon, add the length of all the sides.

Example

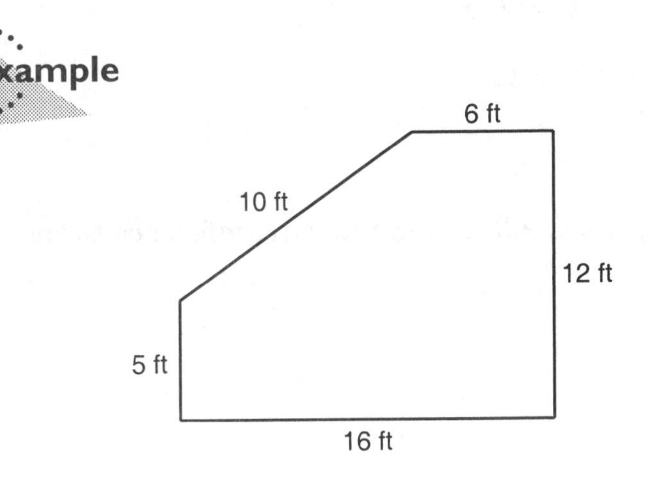

$P = s_1 + s_2 + s_3 \ldots$

$P = 10 + 6 + 12 + 16 + 5$

$P = 49$ ft

The following formulas can be used to find the perimeters of different polygons.

- any polygon (such as the example above): $\boldsymbol{P = s_1 + s_2 + s_3 \ldots}$
- regular polygon ($\boldsymbol{l}$ is length)

  $P = l$ • number of sides

  $P = 6 \bullet 7$

  $P = 42$ in.

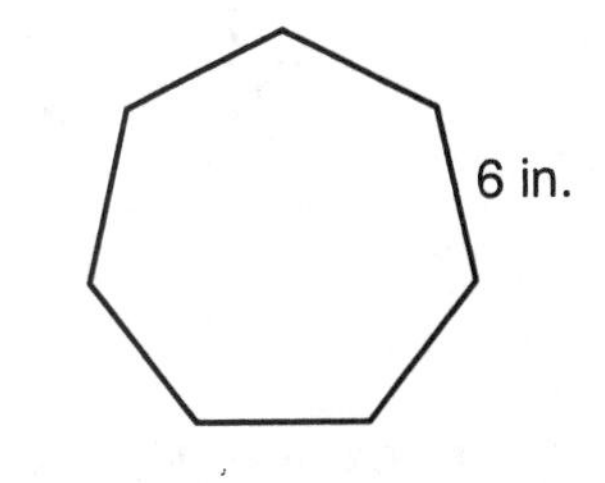

- rectangle or parallelogram

  $\boldsymbol{P = 2l + 2w}$

  $P = 2(22) + 2(8)$

  $P = 44 + 16$

  $P = 60$ cm

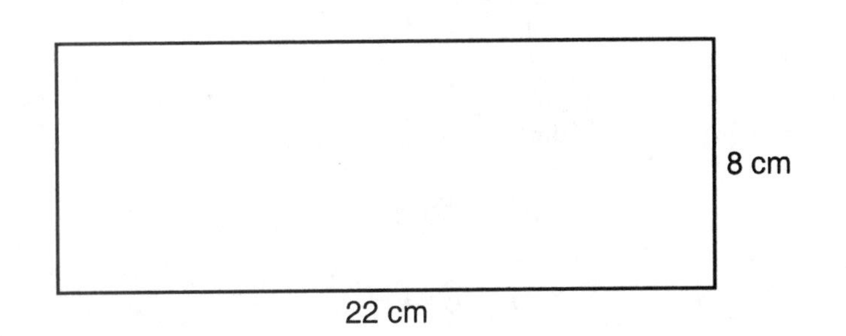

Circumference

Circumference is the distance around the outside of a circle. The formula for circumference is

$$C = \pi d \qquad \text{or} \qquad C = 2\pi r$$

where d = diameter, r = radius, and $\pi \approx 3.14$.

Example

The diameter of a can of peas is 9.3 in. Find its circumference to the nearest tenth.

$C = \pi d$

$C = (3.14)(9.3)$

$C \approx 29.2$ in.

Arc Length

Arc length is a section of a circle's circumference. The length of an arc is related to the size of the angle that forms the arc. Because there are 360° in a circle, the length of an arc is proportional to the circumference in the same way that the angle forming the arc is proportional to 360°.

$$\frac{\text{arc length}}{\text{circumference}} = \frac{\text{angle forming arc}}{360°}$$

$$\frac{\mathbf{l}}{\mathbf{2\pi r}} = \frac{\mathbf{m}}{\mathbf{360°}}$$

Example

Find the arc length. (Use 3.14 for π.)

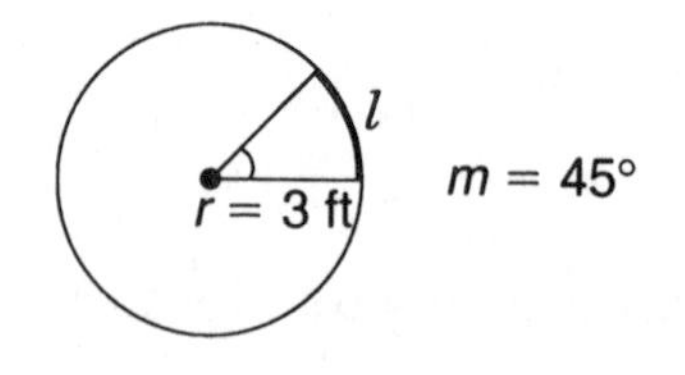

$\frac{l}{2\pi r} = \frac{m}{360°}$

$\frac{l}{18.84} = \frac{1}{8}$

$8l = 18.84$

$l = 2.355$

$l \approx 2.36$ ft

1. What is the circumference of this bicycle wheel? ______________

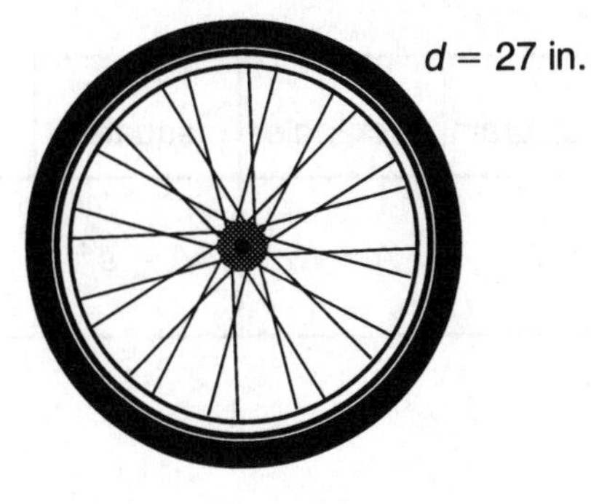

2. Trudy has a mileage meter that counts how many revolutions her bicycle tire makes. About how many revolutions of a wheel with a diameter of 27 inches will equal a mile? (1 mile = 5,280 ft)

3. What is the length of the arc pictured below? Use 3.14 for π. (Round to the nearest whole number.)

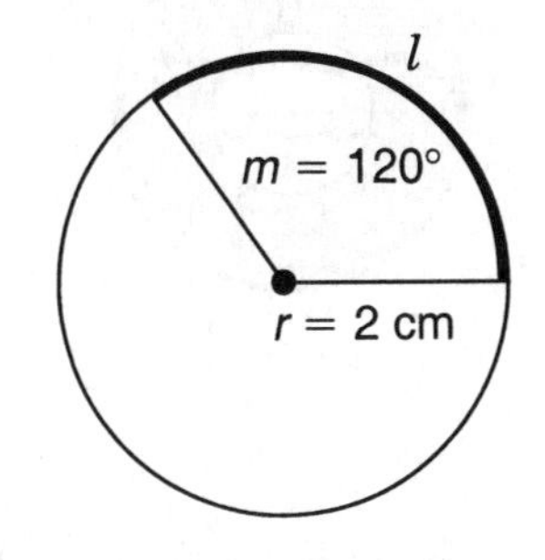

Area

Area is the measure of the region inside a closed plane figure. Area is measured in square units. Use the table below to help you answer the Practice questions.

Name	triangle	parallelogram	rectangle	square	trapezoid	circle
Formula	$A = \frac{1}{2}bh$	$A = bh$	$A = lw$	$A = s^2$	$A = \frac{1}{2}h(b_1 + b_2)$	$A = \pi r^2$

1. What is the approximate area of a jumbo chocolate chip cookie with a diameter of about 5 in.? Use 3.14 for π. (Round to the nearest tenth.)

2. What is the formula for finding the height of a triangle if you are given its base and its area?

3. Find the area of the shaded region.

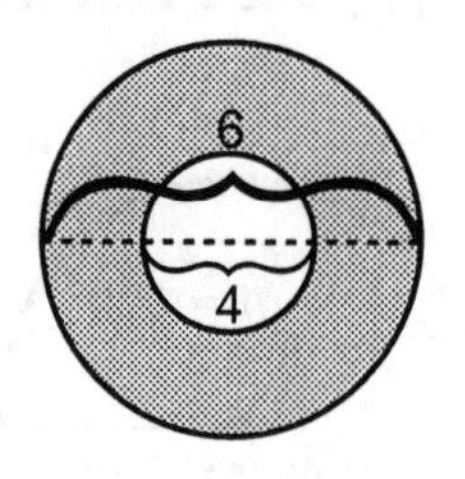

4. How much would it cost to carpet a 12-foot by 9-foot room, if carpet costs \$16.95 a square yard?

Surface Area

Surface area is the measure of the outside surface of a three-dimensional object in square units.

Surface area of rectangular solids

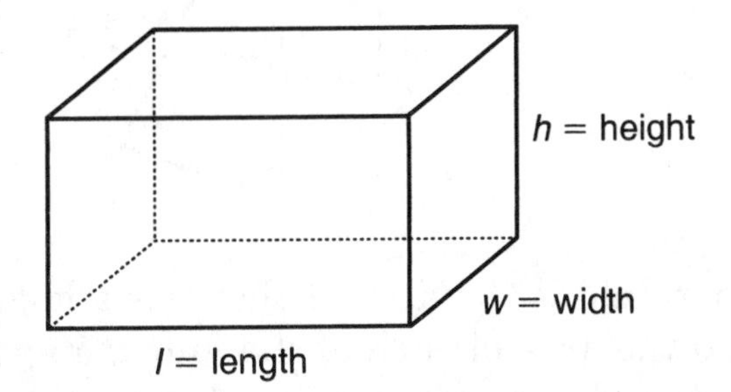

The surface area of a rectangular solid is equal to the sum of the area of each of its faces.

To determine the surface area of a rectangular solid, you can use the formula

$$SA = 2(lw) + 2(hw) + 2(lh)$$

What is the surface area of this rectangular prism?

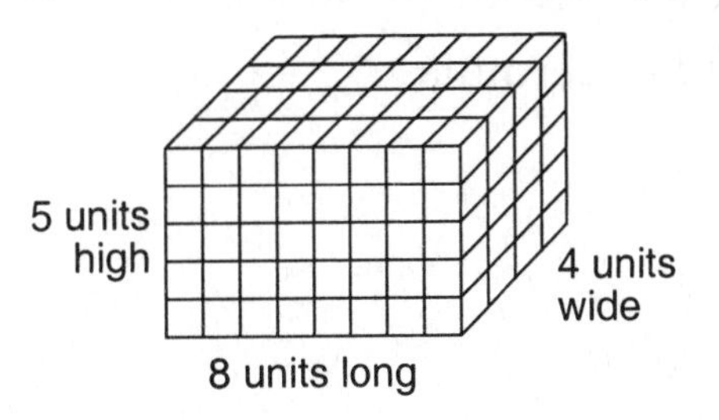

Step 1: **Find the area of the top and the bottom faces.**

$2(lw) = 2(8 \bullet 4) = 64 \text{ units}^2$

Step 2: **Find the area of the left and right faces.**

$2(hw) = 2(5 \bullet 4) = 40 \text{ units}^2$

Step 3: **Find the area of the front and back faces.**

$2(lh) = 2(8 \bullet 5) = 80 \text{ units}^2$

Step 4: **Add the areas of all the faces.**

$64 + 40 + 80 = 184 \text{ units}^2$

Surface area of a pyramid

Below is a square **pyramid** (a pyramid having a square base).

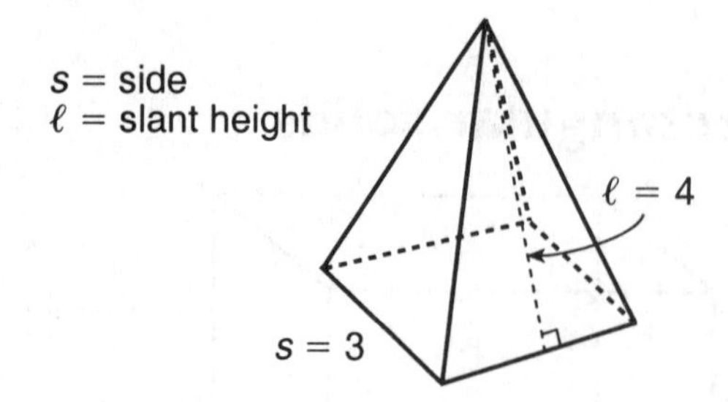

The surface area of a pyramid is the area of the base added to the area of each of the four faces. To find the area of each of the four triangular faces, you need the slant height ℓ, which is the length of a line drawn from the vertex of the pyramid to the middle of a side.

To determine the surface area of a square pyramid, you can use the formula

$$4\left(\frac{1}{2}s\ell\right) + s^2 \qquad \text{or} \qquad 2s\ell + s^2$$

Example

What is the surface area of the pyramid above?

Apply the simplified formula.

$2s\ell + s^2$

$= 2(3 \bullet 4) + 3^2$

$= 2(12) + 9$

$= 24 + 9$

$= 33$

The surface area is 33 square units.

Surface area of a cylinder

The surface area of a **right circular cylinder** is the area of the two circular bases added to the lateral area.

To determine the surface area of a right circular cylinder, you can use the formula $\mathbf{2\pi rh + 2\pi r^2}$.

Example

The formula makes more sense if you "unravel" the cylinder and look at its individual parts.

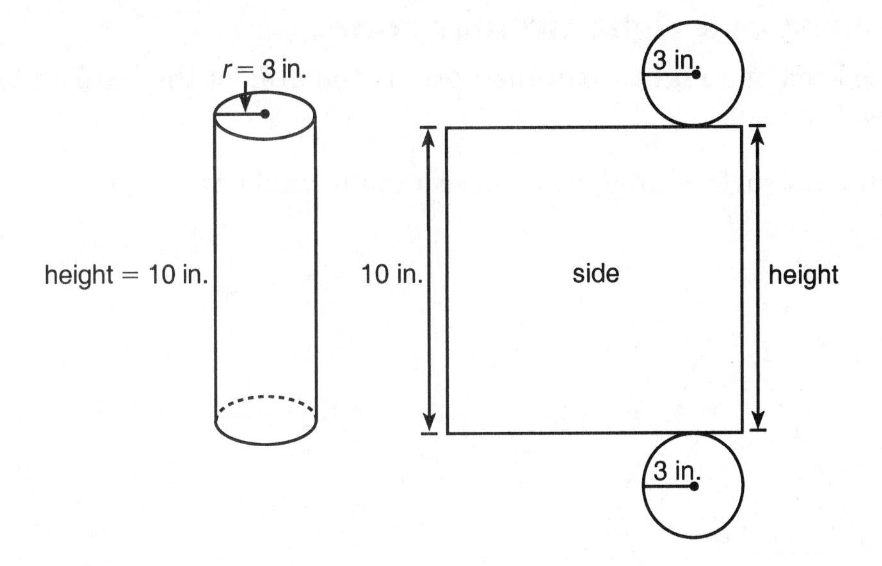

Step 1: **Find the lateral area: $2\pi rh$**

$2(3.14 \bullet 3 \bullet 10)$

$2(94.2) = 188.4$ sq in.

Step 2: **Find the area of the circular bases: $2\pi r^2$**

$2(3.14 \bullet 3^2)$

$2(3.14 \bullet 9)$

$2(28.26) = 56.52$ sq in.

Step 3: **Add the area of the circular bases to the lateral area.**

$188.4 + 56.52 = 244.92$ sq in.

Surface area of a sphere

To determine the surface area of a sphere, you can use the formula $\mathbf{4\pi r^2}$.

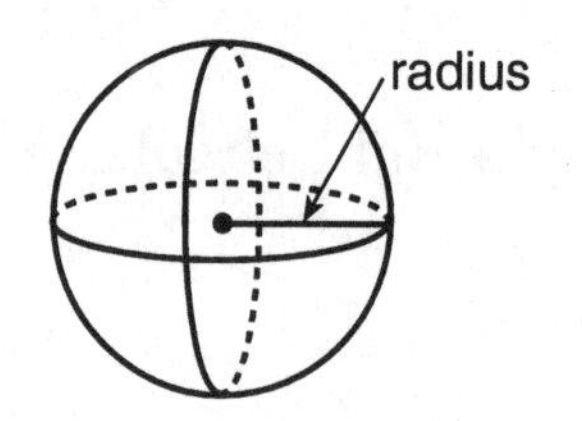

Surface area of a right circular cone

The surface area of a **right circular cone** is the area of the base added to the lateral area.

To determine its surface area, you can use the formula $\boldsymbol{\pi r\ell + \pi r^2}$

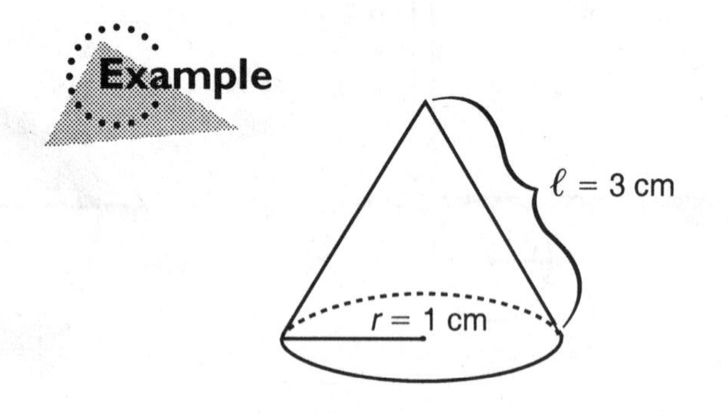

What is the surface area of the cone shown above?

Step 1: **Find the lateral area:** $\boldsymbol{\pi r\ell}$

$3.14 \bullet 1 \bullet 3 = 9.42 \text{ cm}^2$

Step 2: **Find the area of the base:** $\boldsymbol{\pi r^2}$

$3.14 \bullet 12 = 3.14 \text{ cm}^2$

Step 3: **Add the lateral area and the area of the base.**

$9.42 + 3.14 = 12.56 \text{ cm}^2$

Practice

Directions: Find the surface area of the following figures.

1. What is the surface area of this hockey puck? ____________________

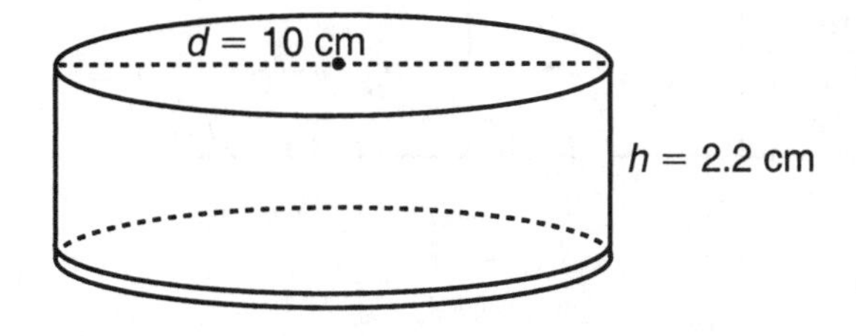

2. What is the surface area of the pyramid shown below? ______________

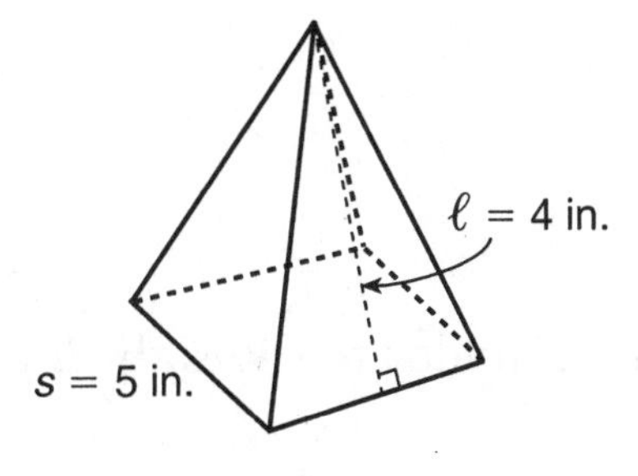

3. How much foil is needed to cover the cone shown below? ____________
(Do not include area of base.)

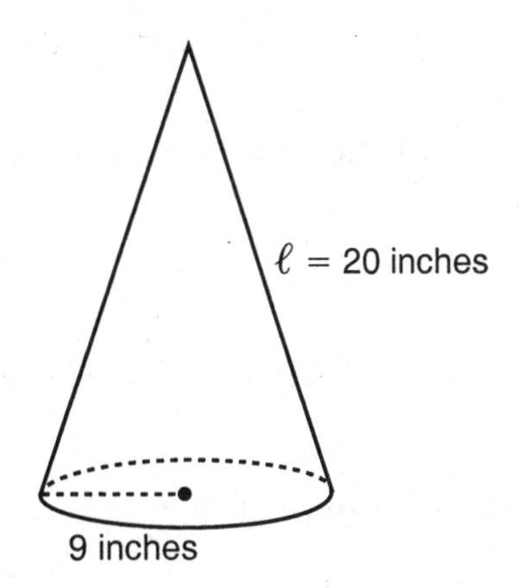

Volume

Volume is the measure of cubic units it takes to fill a space. Use the table below to help you answer the Practice questions.

Name	regular pyramid	regular prism	cylinder	cone	sphere
Formula	$V = Bh$ where $B = lw$	$V = \frac{1}{3}Bh$	$V = \pi r^2 h$	$V = \frac{1}{3}\pi r^2 h$	$V = \frac{4}{3}\pi r^3$

1. What is the height of this model of an Egyptian pyramid if the volume = 200 cm^3?

10 cm 10 cm

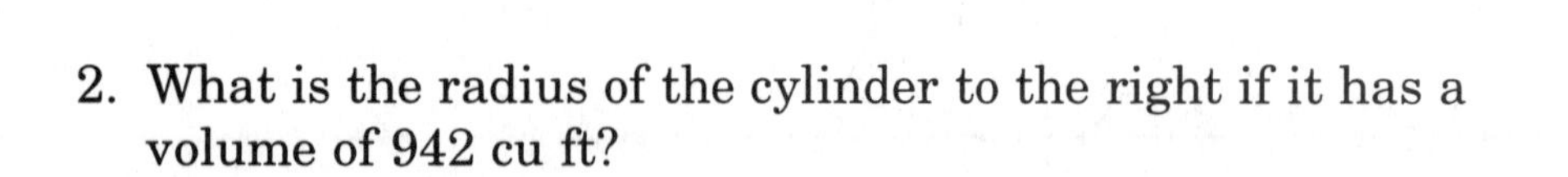

2. What is the radius of the cylinder to the right if it has a volume of 942 cu ft?

h = 12 ft

3. What is the approximate volume of a sphere with a radius of 2.5 m? (Round to the nearest hundredth.)

4. What is the approximate volume of this cone?

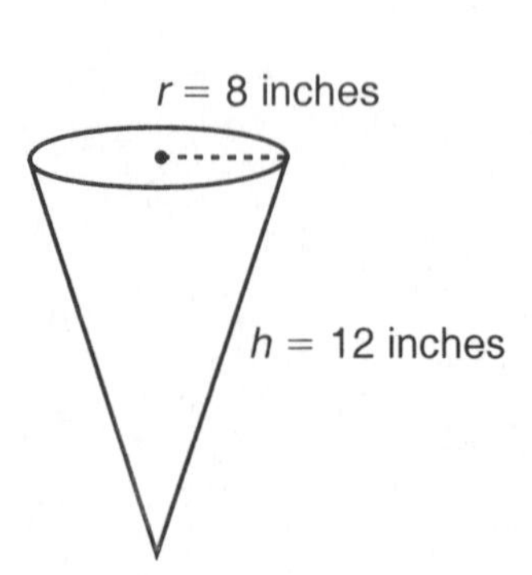

5. Your fish tank has the shape of a rectangular solid. When you added a new rock, the water level rose 0.5 cm. Find the volume of the rock.

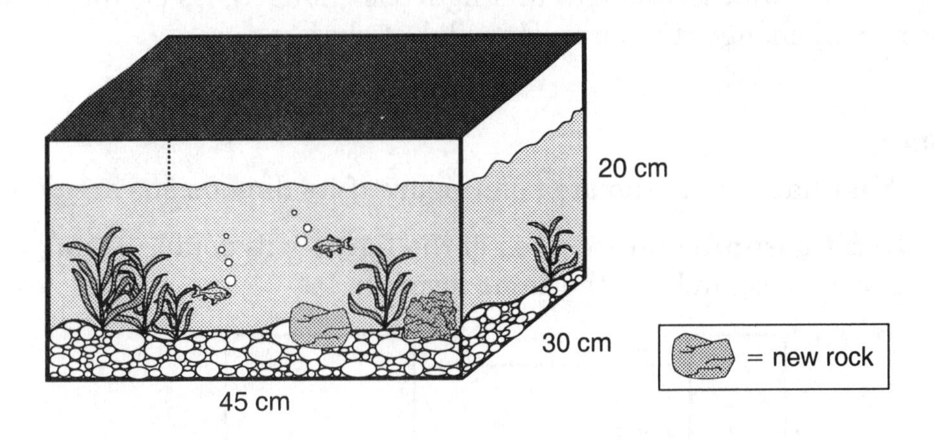

6. A cube has a volume of 64 cm^3. Find the length of its diagonal.

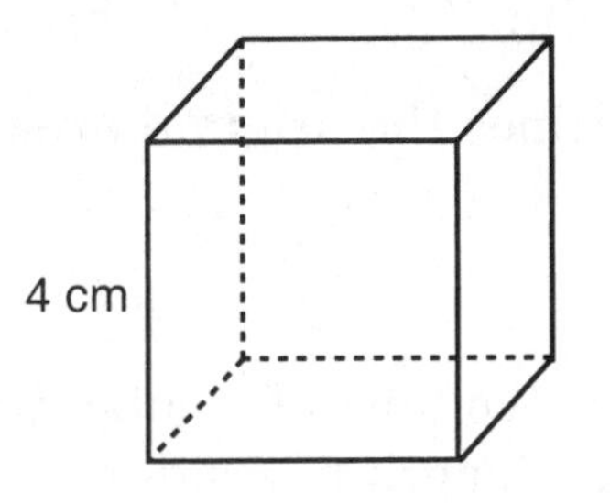

Changes in Dimension

When the length, width, or height of a figure is changed, its perimeter, area, and volume will change (the formulas will not change).

Example

What happens to the area of a figure if its dimensions are doubled?

Don't assume that the area of the figure will double. Change the dimensions, and use the same formula.

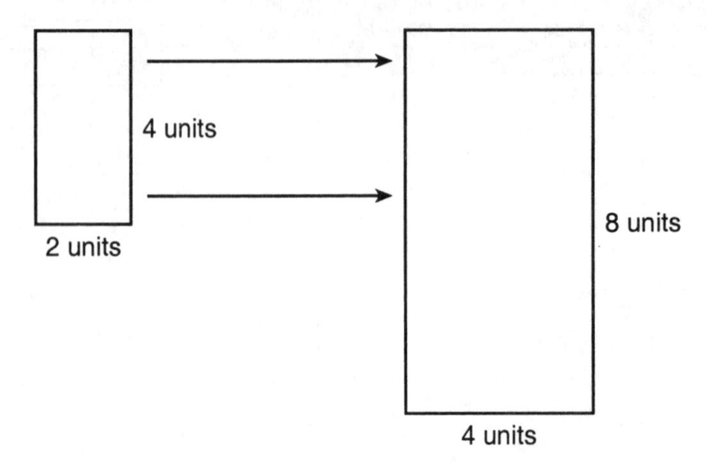

Original Area	**New Area**
length = 4 units	length doubled = 8 units
width = 2 units	width doubled = 4 units
area (lw) = 8 units	area (lw) = 32 units

The new area is 4 times the original area.

Example

What happens to the volume of a cube, whose sides measure 3 in., when you double the length of a side?

Original Volume	**New Volume**
$V = s^3$; $s = 3$ in.	$V = s^3$; $s = 6$ in.
$V = 27$ cu in.	$V = 216$ cu in.

The new volume is 8 times the original volume.

1. What would be the perimeter of the figure below if its length were doubled and its width tripled?

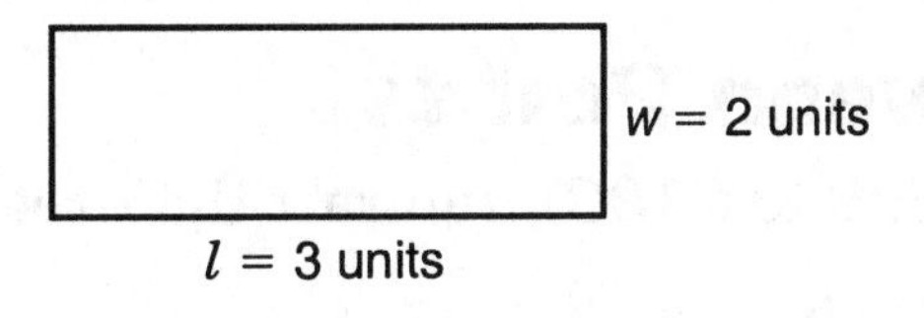

2. What would be the volume of the figure below if all of its dimensions were tripled?

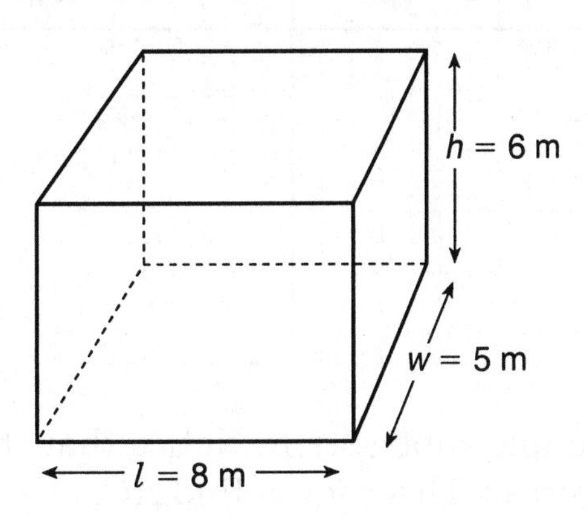

Lesson 9: Geometry from an Algebraic Perspective

This lesson deals with using algebraic methods to solve geometric problems.

Distance Between Points

To find the distance from B to C (BC), subtract the x-coordinates.

$$BC = 8 - 2 = 6$$

To find the distance from B to A (BA), subtract the y-coordinates.

$$BA = 9 - 1 = 8$$

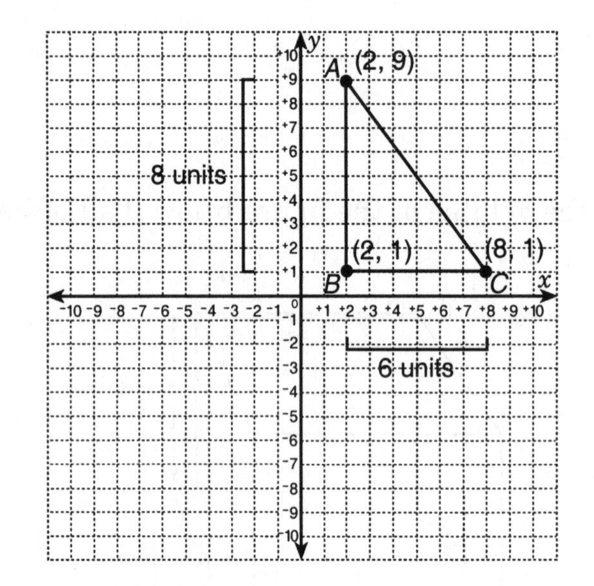

You cannot find AC by simple subtraction. Notice that the figure is a right triangle. Use the Pythagorean Theorem to find AC.

$$(AB)^2 + (BC)^2 = (AC)^2$$

$$\sqrt{(AB)^2 + (BC)^2} = AC$$

$$\sqrt{8^2 + 6^2} = AC$$

$$\sqrt{64 + 36} = AC$$

$$\sqrt{100} = AC$$

$$10 = AC$$

The distance from A to C is 10.

The **distance formula** is similar to the Pythagorean Theorem.

$$d = \sqrt{(x_2 - x_1)^2 + (y_2 - y_1)^2}$$

What are the coordinates of point C? ______________ point A? ______________

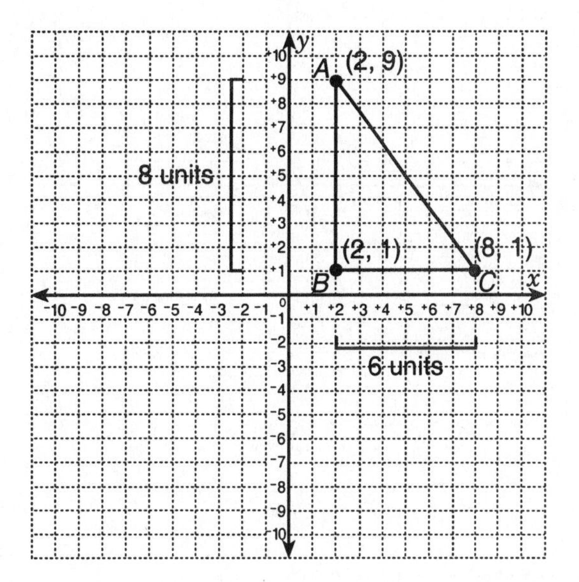

$$d(AC) = \sqrt{(x_2 - x_1)^2 + (y_2 - y_1)^2}$$

$$d(AC) = \sqrt{(8 - 2)^2 + (1 - 9)^2}$$

$$d(AC) = \sqrt{(6)^2 + (^-8)^2}$$

$$= \sqrt{36 + 64}$$

$$= \sqrt{100}$$

$$d(AC) = 10$$

Practice

Directions: Use the parallelogram $ABCD$ to answer Numbers 1 through 4.

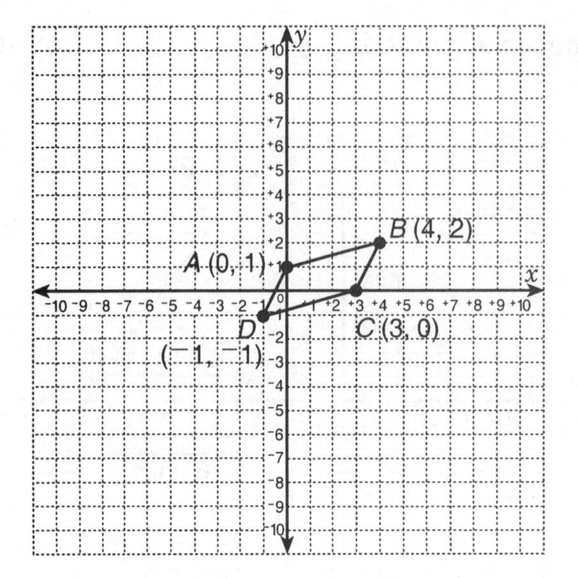

1. AB = ______________________

2. DC = ______________________

3. AD = ______________________

4. BC = ______________________

5. Using what you know about parallelograms, justify the relationship of the distances in Numbers 1 through 4.

____

____

____

____

____

Midpoint

The **midpoint** is the point that divides a segment into two equal segments.

$$P_1 = (x_1, y_1) \text{ and } P_2 = (x_2, y_2)$$

You can think of the midpoint as the **average** of the two endpoints.

The midpoint of a line segment can be found with the formula

$$M = \left(\frac{x_2 + x_1}{2}, \frac{y_2 + y_1}{2}\right)$$

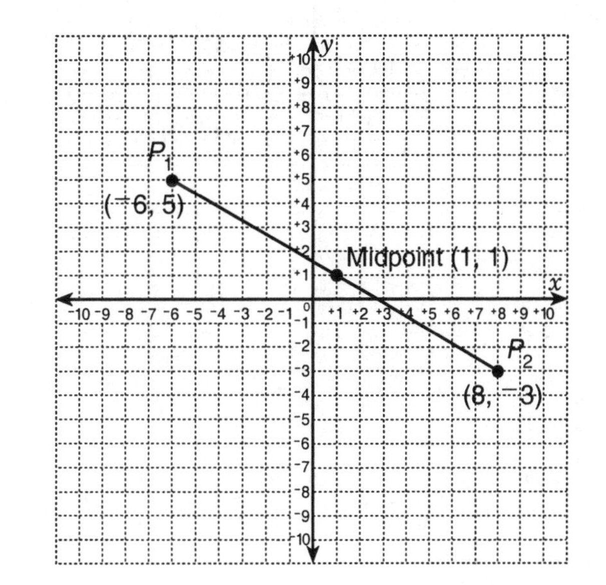

$$M = \left(\frac{x_2 + x_1}{2}, \frac{y_2 + y_1}{2}\right)$$

$$M = \left(\frac{8 + (^-6)}{2}, \frac{^-3 + 5}{2}\right)$$

$$= \left(\frac{2}{2}, \frac{2}{2}\right)$$

$$= (1, 1)$$

Practice

Directions: Use the parallelogram *ABCD* to find the midpoint of the sides in Numbers 1 through 4.

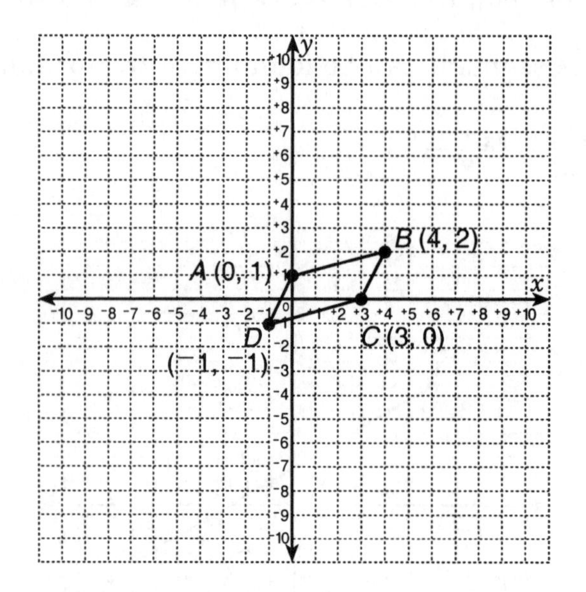

1. Side *AB* ____________________

2. Side *AD* ____________________

3. Side *BC* ____________________

4. Side *CD* ____________________

Congruency and Similarity

Congruent figures

Two figures are congruent if their corresponding angles and sides are congruent.

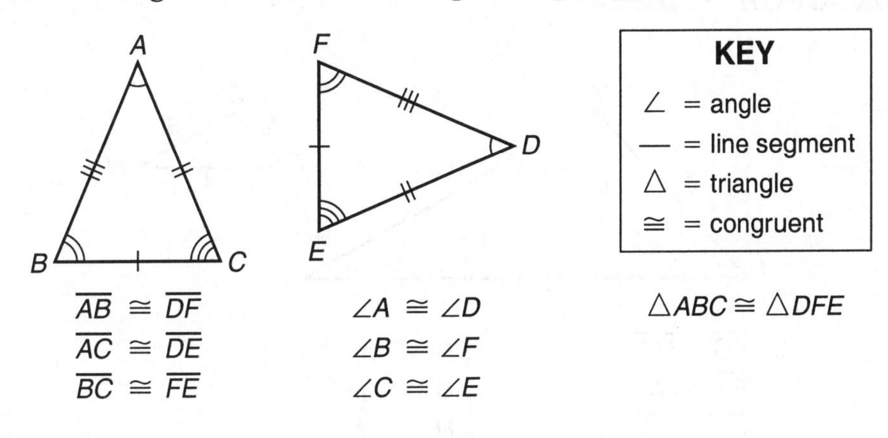

ABCDEF ≅ *JKLMNO*

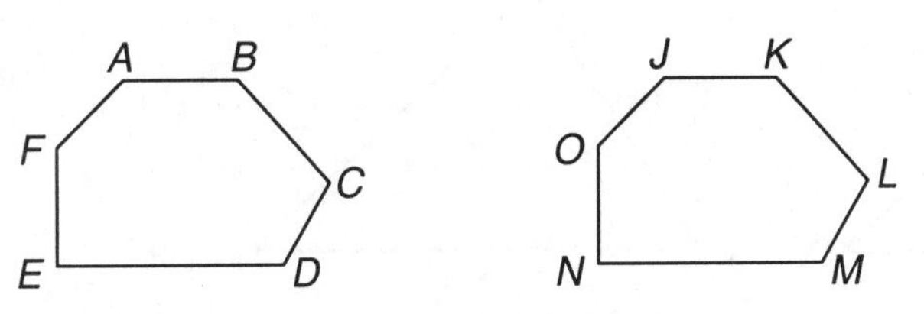

1. Which angle in *ABCDEF* is congruent with $\angle M$? ____________________

2. Name two pairs of congruent sides. ____________________

____

3. Name two other pairs of congruent angles. ____________________

____

Similarity

Figures that have the same shape but not the same size are **similar figures**. The symbol for similar is ~.

For example: $\triangle FGH \sim \triangle LMN$

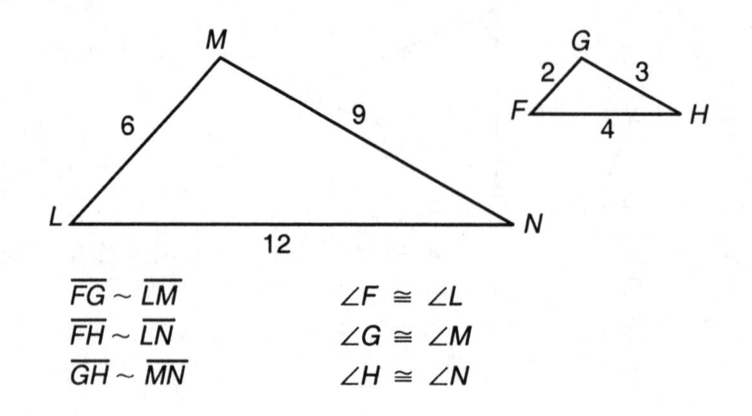

The length of the sides of similar figures are proportional.

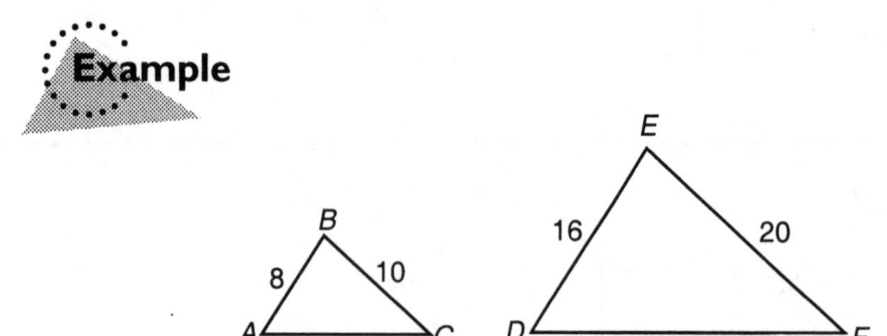

$\triangle ABC \sim \triangle DEF$. Find the length of side x.

$$\frac{8}{12} = \frac{12}{x}$$

$$8x = 192$$

$$x = 24$$

1. In the grid below,
   A. plot the following coordinates and label each point:
      $W = (^-3, ^-2)$, $X = (^-2, 3)$, $Y = (3, 3)$, and $Z = (2, ^-2)$.
   B. draw a line connecting the points in order from W to Z ending up back at W.
   C. draw a figure similar to figure $WXYZ$.

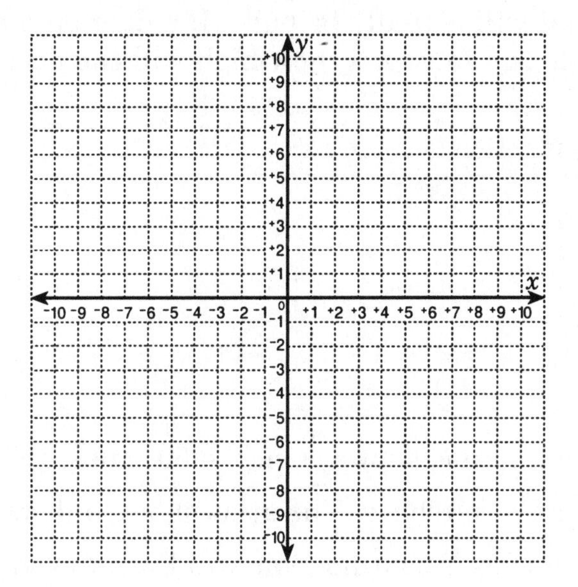

Directions: Solve for x in Numbers 2 and 3.

2. $\triangle LMN \sim \triangle RST$

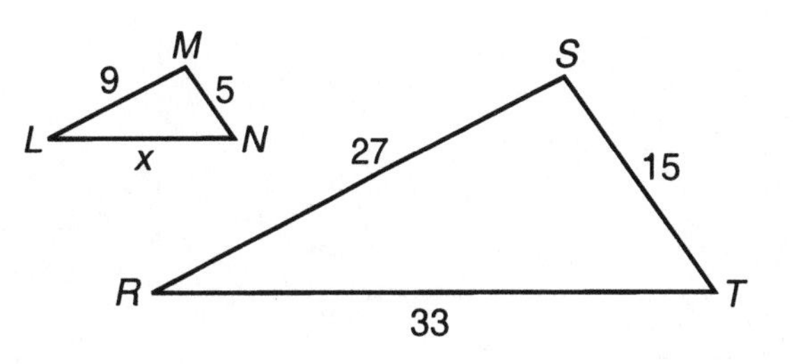

3. $\triangle ABCDE \sim \triangle FGHIJ$

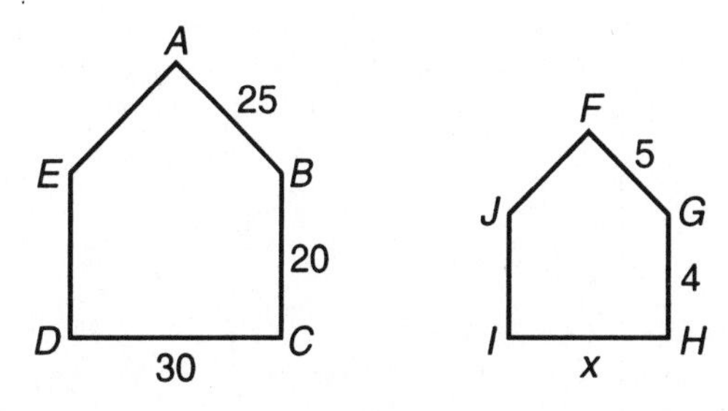

Scale

Scale drawings show objects in direct proportion to their actual size.

Practice

1. Architects use scale models and drawings to represent what an actual house or building will look like. All parts of the scale model are in proportion to what will actually be built. If a door on a scale model is 4 in. high and the scale is 1 in. = 2 ft, how high will the door on the actual house be?

   ____

2. The scale on Frank's atlas shows $\frac{1}{2}$ inch = 50 miles. He is planning a trip from Ida Grove to Parkersburg. The atlas shows a distance of approximately 3 inches. About how far will Frank need to travel for a round-trip?

   ____

3. Marcia is drawing her house and family to scale. Her scale is 1 inch = 3 feet. In real life, her father is 6 feet tall. Her dog is 2 feet tall. How tall will she need to draw her father and dog?

   ____

Transformations and Symmetry

Translations, reflections, and rotations are ways in which a figure can be transformed. Each one of these transformations also refers to a kind of symmetry.

Translation (Slide)

When you move a figure without changing anything other than its position, it is called a **translation**, or a **slide**. Figures can be slid in any direction.

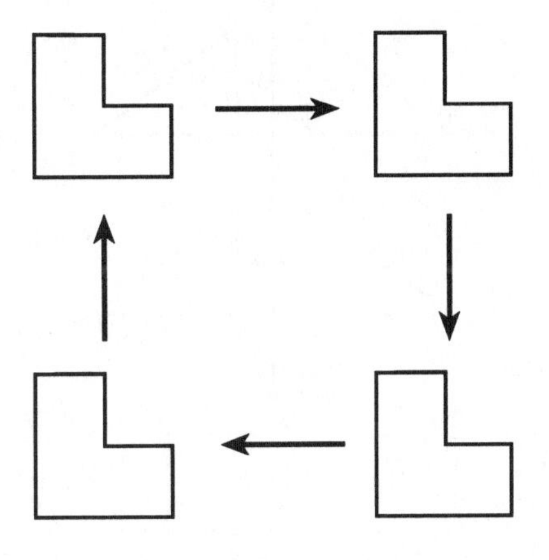

Translational symmetry

If you can slide a figure a certain distance in a given direction so that it lands on top of an identical figure, the two are said to have **translational symmetry**. Sometimes this can continue on in a pattern with any number of identical figures lined up at equal distances apart.

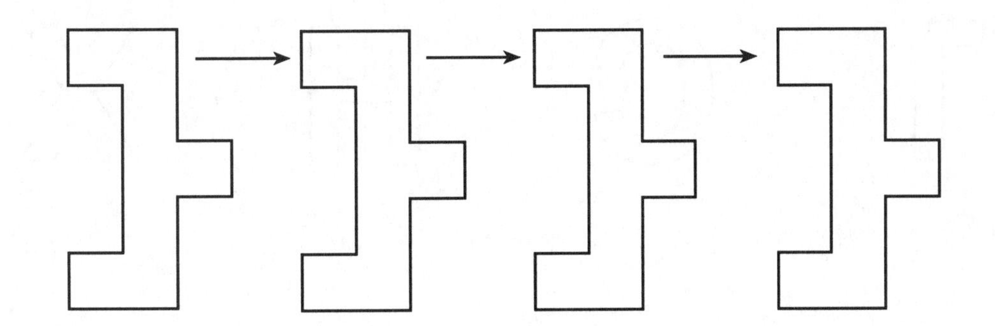

Reflection

When you flip a figure and create its mirror image, you have performed a **reflection**. When a figure is reflected, there must be a **line of reflection**, or a **line of symmetry**. When you are asked to identify or draw the reflection of a figure, this line must be given.

In the following example, triangle 2 is a reflection of triangle 1, and triangle 3 is a reflection of triangle 4. The line of symmetry is the vertical line labeled y.

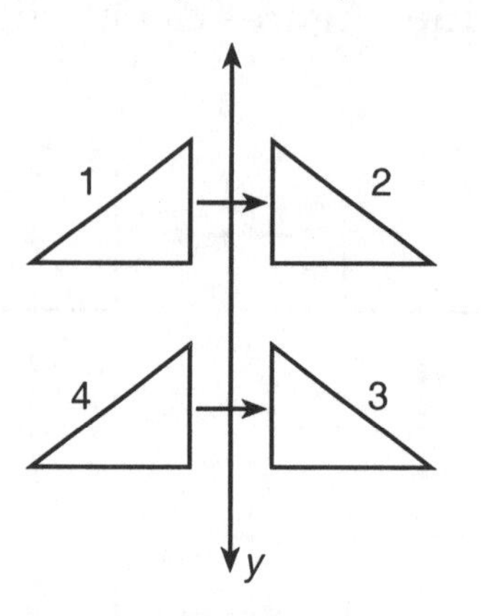

Reflectional symmetry

A figure has **reflectional symmetry** if there is a line of reflection through it, and its two halves are mirror images of each other. Sometimes a figure has reflectional symmetry in more than one direction. Reflectional symmetry is also known as **line symmetry**, **bilateral symmetry**, and **mirror symmetry**.

Letters are good examples of figures with reflectional symmetry. The dotted lines represent lines of symmetry.

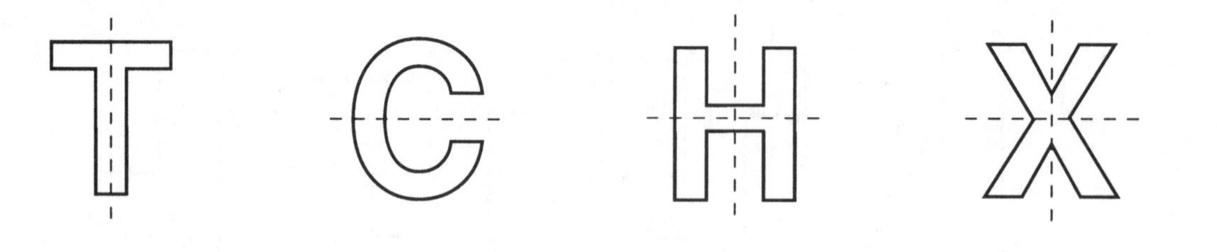

Rotation

When you turn a figure about a certain point, a **rotation** has been performed. A $\frac{1}{4}$ turn is the same as rotating 90°, $\frac{1}{2}$ turn = 180°, and $\frac{3}{4}$ turn = 270°. A full turn is equal to 360°. You must identify the center of rotation with a point, and specify a clockwise or counterclockwise direction. The figures below show clockwise rotations.

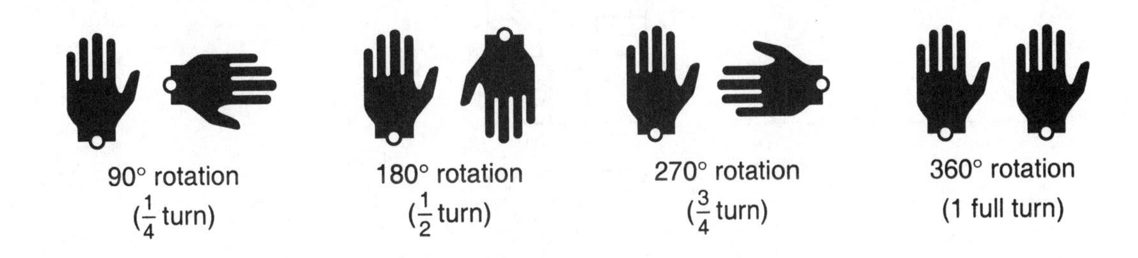

Rotational symmetry

If a figure can be rotated less than 360° around its point of rotation, so that it coincides with its original image, it is said to have **rotational symmetry**. The figure below has rotational symmetry about point G.

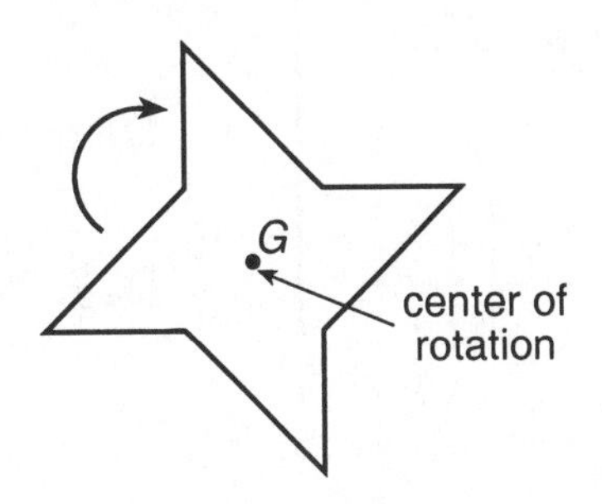

Asymmetry

Shapes that have **no symmetry** are called asymmetric. Each of the following figures is asymmetric.

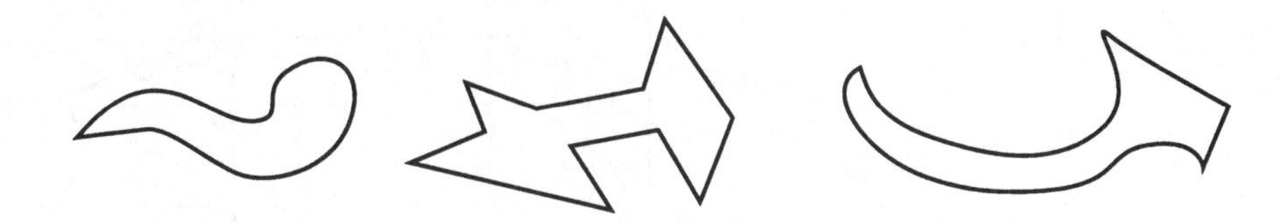

Directions: Identify the type or types of symmetry found in each figure or pattern for Numbers 1 through 3.

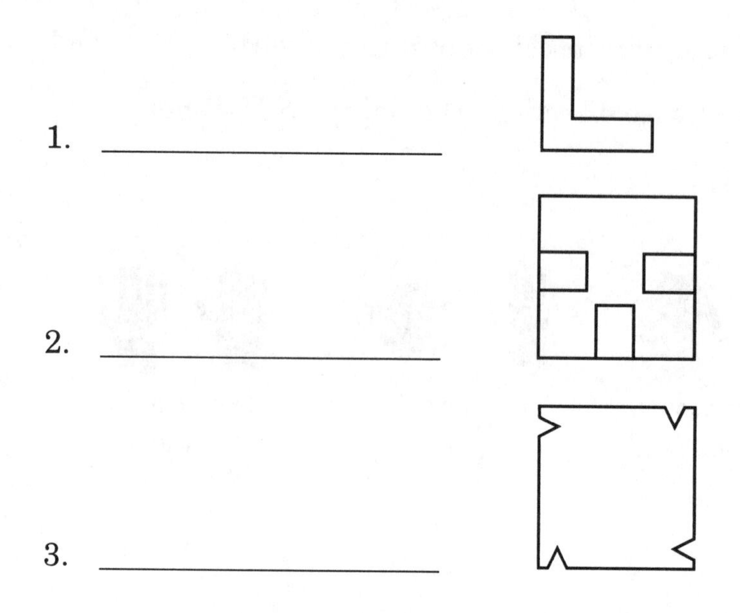

1. ____________________

2. ____________________

3. ____________________

4. Translate figure $EFGH$ nine coordinates to the left and seven coordinates up. What are the new coordinates of rectangle $EFGH$?

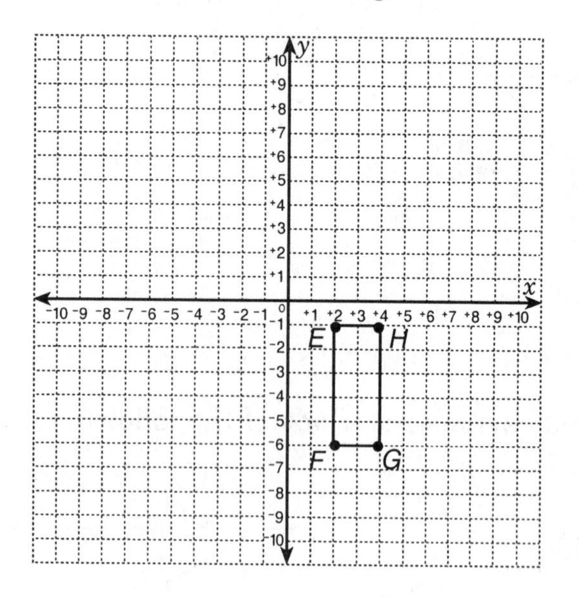

5. Name two ways you could rotate $\triangle CDE$ about $(^-4, ^-2)$ so that it completely covers $\triangle STU$.

Degree of turn: ________ clockwise

Degree of turn: ________ counter-clockwise

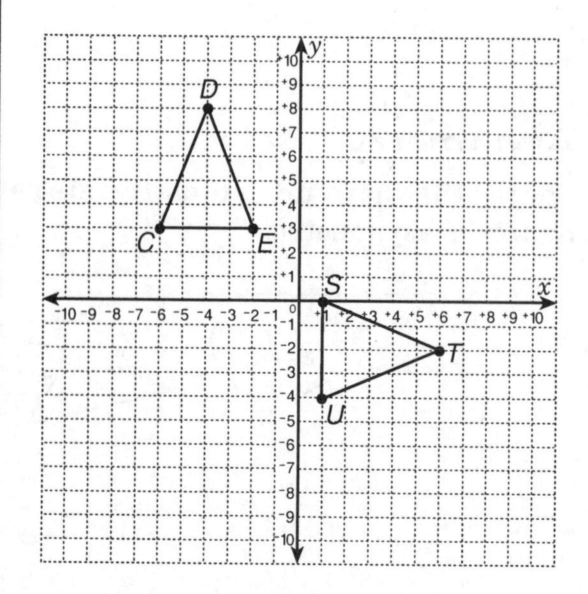

Tessellations

A **tessellation** is a combination of one or more shapes that completely covers a plane in a repeating pattern, with no spaces or gaps between shapes and no shapes overlapping.

A **regular tessellation** is made of regular polygons. The three regular polygons that can tessellate are equilateral triangles, squares, and regular hexagons.

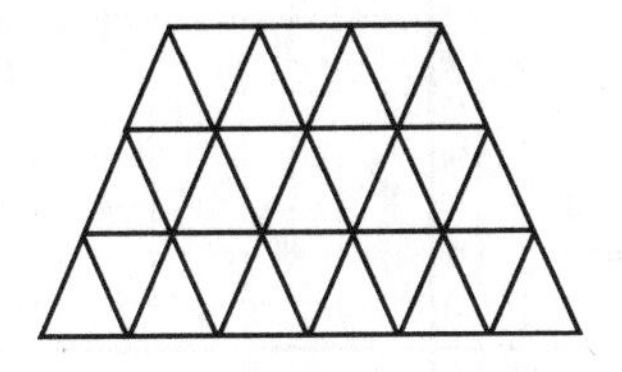

equilateral triangles

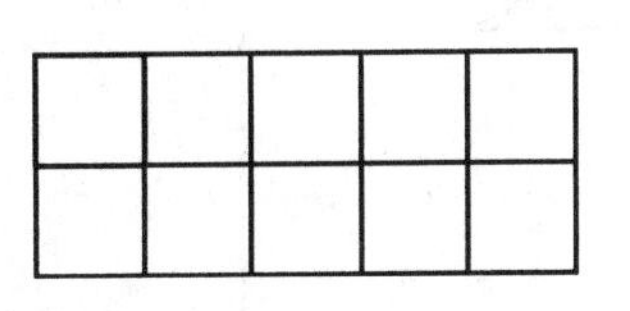

squares

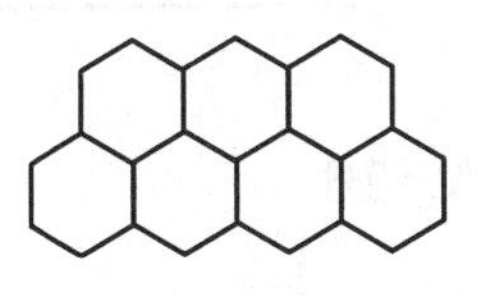

regular hexagons

A **semiregular tessellation** is composed of two or more regular polygons that combine to form a repeating pattern.

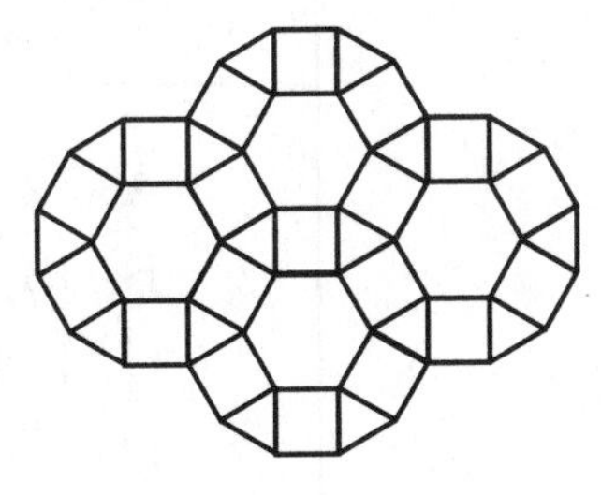

1. Continue the tessellation on the graph until it reaches or passes (2, $^-6$).

2. Will the point (2, $^-6$) be inside a polygon or on the line of a polygon?

____

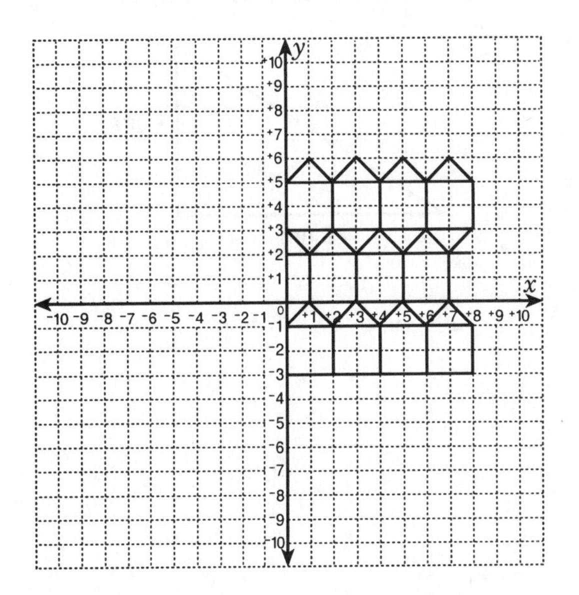

Test Your Skills

1. What is the value of x?

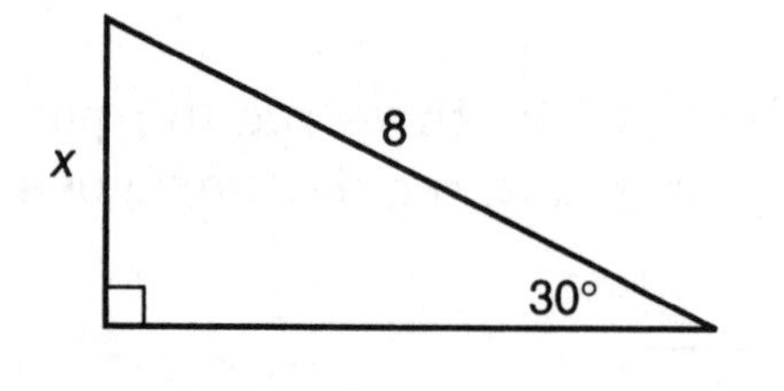

A. 16

B. $8\sqrt{3}$

C. $8\sqrt{3} \div 3$

D. 4

2. What is the length, rounded to the nearest hundredth, of c?

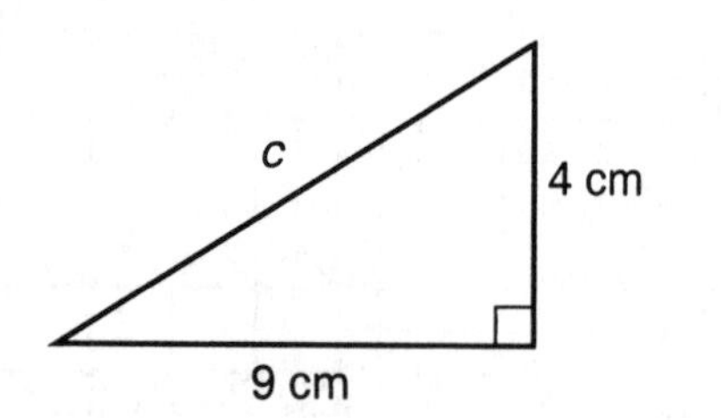

3. What are the coordinates of point H?

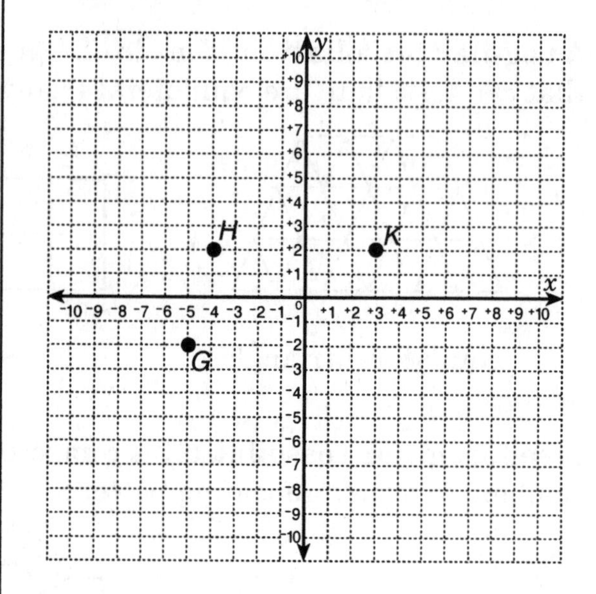

A. (2, $^{-}4$)

B. (3, 2)

C. ($^{-}4$, 2)

D. ($^{-}5$, $^{-}2$)

4. Nora lives 8 miles north of Oakdale Mall and Jill lives 9 miles west of Nora. If there is a direct diagonal route from the mall to Jill's house, how far do Nora and Jill have to travel to get to the mall from Jill's house? Round your answer to the nearest hundredth.

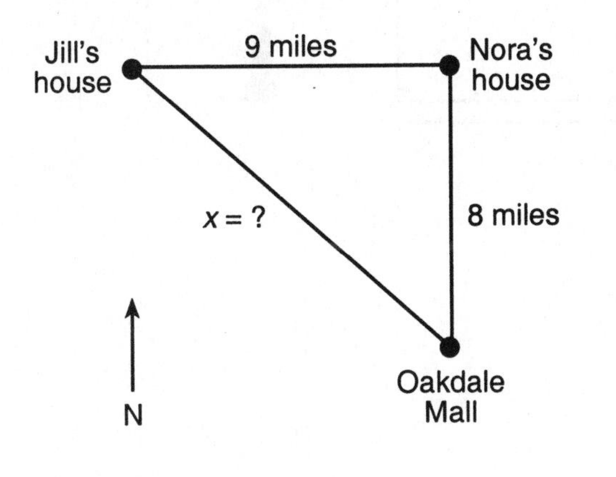

5. What is the measure in degrees of angle *m*?

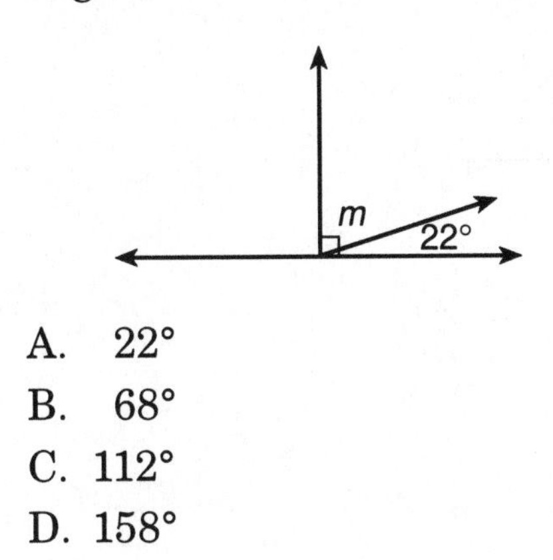

A. 22°
B. 68°
C. 112°
D. 158°

6. Which two angles in the figure are supplementary?

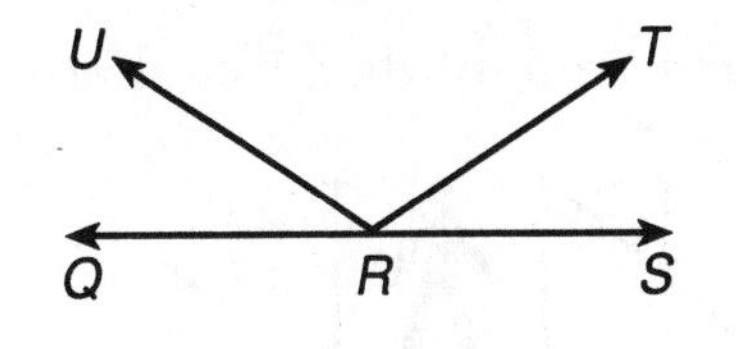

A. $\angle SRT$ and $\angle QRU$
B. $\angle QRS$ and $\angle SRT$
C. $\angle QRU$ and $\angle QRT$
D. $\angle QRT$ and $\angle SRT$

7. Draw a translation and a clockwise rotation of the figure below. Label the point of rotation.

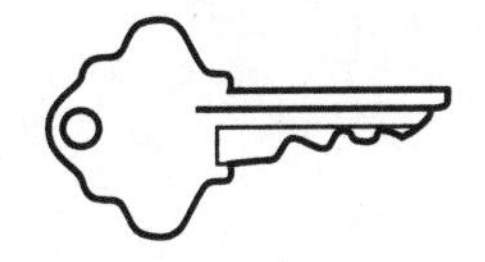

8. Seth wants to know the height of the tree in his front yard. At a certain time of day, the tree's shadow is 63 feet long. Seth is $5\frac{1}{2}$ feet tall and at the same time of day, his shadow is 7 feet long. How tall is the tree? ________

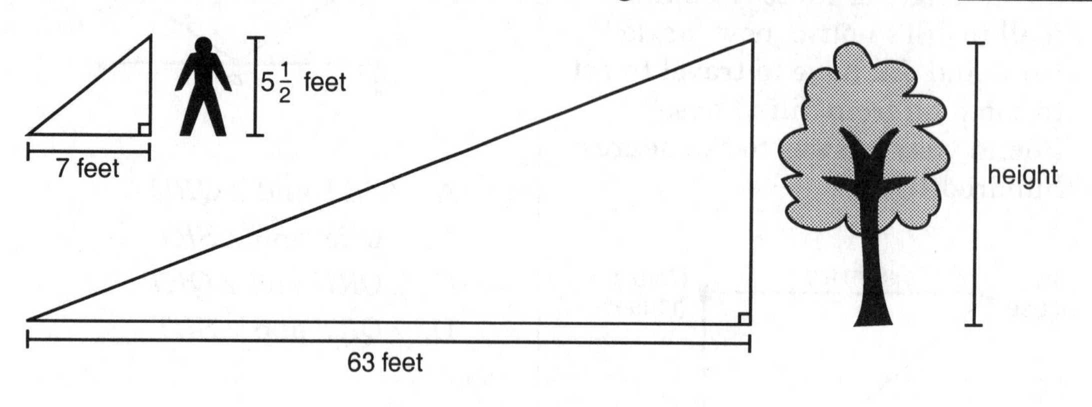

9. Everyone in town walks diagonally across Samantha's lawn. Samantha's mother has decided to make a garden in the triangle between the two sides of the sidewalk and the path. What is the area of her garden bed in square feet?

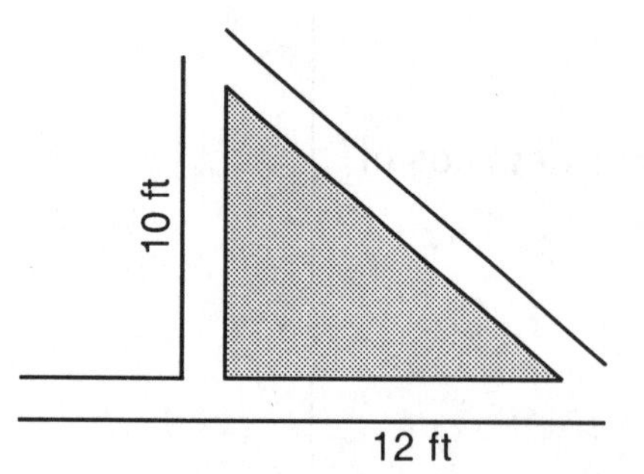

A. 60 sq ft
B. 40 sq ft
C. 22 sq ft
D. 6.6 sq ft

10. Jenny and her friends are getting ready to go camping. On the road map, it is $2\frac{1}{3}$ inches from Boston to Worcester and another 2 inches from Worcester to the campground. Jenny knows that it is 42 miles from Boston to Worcester. How many miles is the drive to the campground from Boston?
    A. 36 miles
    B. 49 miles
    C. 54 miles
    D. 78 miles

11. For a high school play, the properties manager wants to cover tin cans with old-fashioned labels. How long should the labels be, to the nearest centimeter?

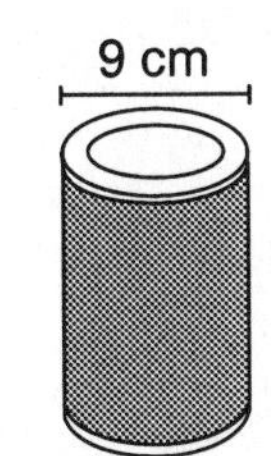

    A. 47
    B. 28
    C. 15
    D. 9

12. The women's softball league uses a 14 inch circumference ball. The men's league uses a 15 inch circumference ball. What is the ratio, in terms of volume, of the women's softball to the men's softball? (Round to the nearest whole number.)

____

13. A glass 2 inches in diameter and 4 inches tall can hold how many cubic inches of liquid?
    A. 4π cu in.
    B. 8 cu in.
    C. 12.4π cu in.
    D. 16 cu in.

14. Louie plans to use the athletic department's plastic pylons as molds to make 50 concrete parking lot cones. How many cubic feet of concrete, to the nearest tenth, will the 50 pylons require?

____

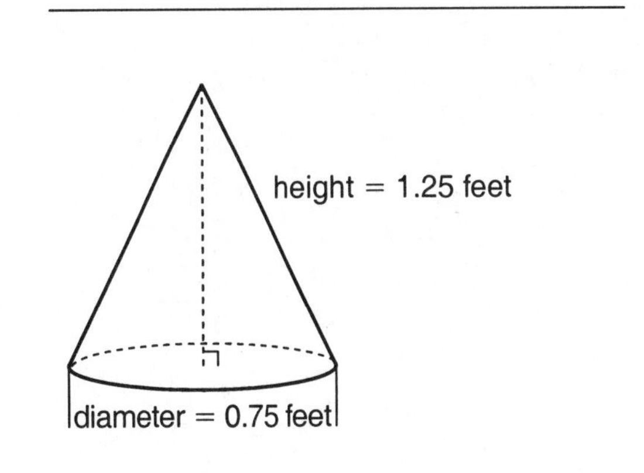

15. A block of ice 12 inches by 8 inches by 24 inches has a surface area of 1,152 square inches. Explain how to find the surface area of an equal volume of ice, if it is separated into 1 inch square cubes. Justify your answer mathematically.

16. A polygon's interior angles add up to 540°. Draw the polygon and explain how you arrived at that particular shape.

UNIT 4

Statistics and Probability

Lesson 10: Statistics

Lesson 11: Probability

Lesson 10: Statistics

Statistics is a set of methods used to collect, organize, describe, and analyze numerical data.

Measures of Central Tendency

Measures of central tendency use one number to represent all the numbers in the set.

The **mean**, **median**, and **mode** are the three measures that can be used to describe the central tendency of the data. The information you're looking for determines which measure you should use.

Mean

The **mean** is the sum of the numbers in a group divided by how many numbers are in that group. It is affected by all the numbers in the set.

Median

The **median** is the middle number in a group of numbers arranged in order of value.

Mode

The **mode** is the number that appears most often in a set of numbers.

Directions: Using the table below, find the mean, median, and mode for this set of scores.

Scores on English Tests

Student	1	2	3	4	5	6	7	8
Test 1	69	82	79	82	70	70	85	87

1. Mean = ______________

2. Median = ______________

3. Mode = ______________

Measures of Dispersion

Measures of dispersion, also called measures of **variability**, describe data sets by telling us how much the numbers vary, or differ, from each other.

Here, we will focus on the **range**. To find the range, find the difference between the largest and smallest number in the set of data.

The range of the English test scores (on the preceding page) is 18. (87 – 69).

Practice

Directions: Use the following tables to answer Numbers 1 through 4.

Home Runs Hit Per Month

Month	Martínez	Jackson
April	0	4
May	10	5
June	1	5
July	5	5
August	5	6
September	9	5
TOTAL	30	30

	Mode	Median	Mean
Martínez	5	5	5
Jackson	5	5	5

1. What is the range for Martínez? ______________

2. What is the range for Jackson? ______________

3. Whose data shows more variability? ______________

4. What does the range help explain that the mean, median, and mode do not?

____

____

____

Collecting Data: Samples and Surveys

Using statistical methods, we can make predictions for a large group on the basis of data collected from a subgroup.

The large group is called a **population**. The subgroup drawn from the large group is called a **sample**. The collected data from a subgroup is a **survey**.

Since it is almost impossible, for example, to call all of the registered voters in Massachusetts in a telephone poll, a sample is drawn from the total population.

It is very important that a sample be **random** and **sufficiently large**. Sample bias is a source of error caused by using improper methods for selecting a sample.

Practice

Directions: Identify whether the situations in Numbers 1 through 3 would provide a random or biased sample.

1. Determining the yearly rainfall in Massachusetts by measuring the yearly rainfall in Boston.

   ____

2. Determining the most popular type of motorcycle in your town by calling people listed on the 100th page of the telephone book.

   ____

3. Determining the type of toothpaste prefered by most tenth-graders in your town by standing outside the tenth-grade classroom(s) from 7:45 A.M. to 8:45 A.M. and surveying every fifth student entering the classroom(s).

   ____

4. Explain how you would design a survey to conduct at your school to find out the most watched television program on Thursday nights between 8:00 P.M. and 8:30 P.M.

   Population: ______________________________

   Sample: ______________________________

Displaying Data

Graphic displays of numerical data help you summarize information, show trends, make predictions, and draw conclusions. The most common are pictographs, bar graphs, and line graphs.

Frequency distributions

A **frequency distribution** lists data values and the number of times (the frequency) each value occurs.

Example

The list below shows the age at which 30 teachers retired from Monroe High School.

69, 60, 60, 61, 60, 63, 62, 65, 66, 62, 65, 60, 61, 64, 63, 69, 60, 62, 61, 62, 64, 65, 68, 62, 63, 68, 69, 60, 62, 62

The number of tally marks, called the frequencies, are listed in the third column.

Age at Retirement

Age	Tally Marks	Frequency
60	~~IIII~~ I	6
61	IIII	4
62	~~IIII~~ II	7
63	III	3
64	II	2
65	III	3
66	I	1
67		0
68	II	2
69	III	3

The frequencies in a frequency distribution are the bars in a histogram. In a histogram, all the bars are adjacent.

Practice

1. Some students in the 10th grade participated in a bike-a-thon for charity. The frequency table below shows the distance ridden and how many students rode that distance.

10th-Grade Bike-A-Thon

Distance Ridden	Frequency
5 miles	10
10 miles	16
15 miles	14

What was the mean distance ridden? ______________

2. The data below shows the number of push-ups done by the members of Mr. Ryan's gym class. Make a frequency table for this data.

   22, 23, 23, 22, 25, 24, 27, 27,

   25, 25, 21, 22, 21, 22, 25, 30

3. What was the mean number of push-ups done? ______________________

Circle graphs

A **circle graph** shows information at one particular time; it does not show trends or changes over a period of time. The sum of all its parts must equal 100% (or 1).

Practice

The Vesuvio Pie Shop sold 50 pies last week. Use the table below to answer Numbers 1 through 3.

Pies	Number Sold	Percent
Apple	24	48%
Cherry	13	26%
Blueberry	4	8%
Lemon	4	8%
Rhubarb	5	10%
TOTAL	50	100%

1. Fill in the graph with the number of each kind of pie sold as a percentage of the total pies sold.

Vesuvio Pie Shop Sales

2. How many more apple pies would need to be sold to make the apple pie section exactly half of the circle? (Base your answer on a total sale of 50 pies.)

   ____

3. Which sections could you combine to make a section equal to the cherry pie section?

   ____

Line plots

A **line plot** is used when you want to show the spread of the data so that you can quickly identify the range, the mode, and any outliers in the data. **Outliers** are separated from the rest of the data (either very low or very high).

Practice

1. Sixteen 10th-graders estimated the number of hours per week they spent participating in extra curricular school activities. These are the results: 14, 9, 16, 14, 11, 14, 20, 7, 11, 9, 16, 17, 15, 15, 5, 10. Use the line plot below to show these results.

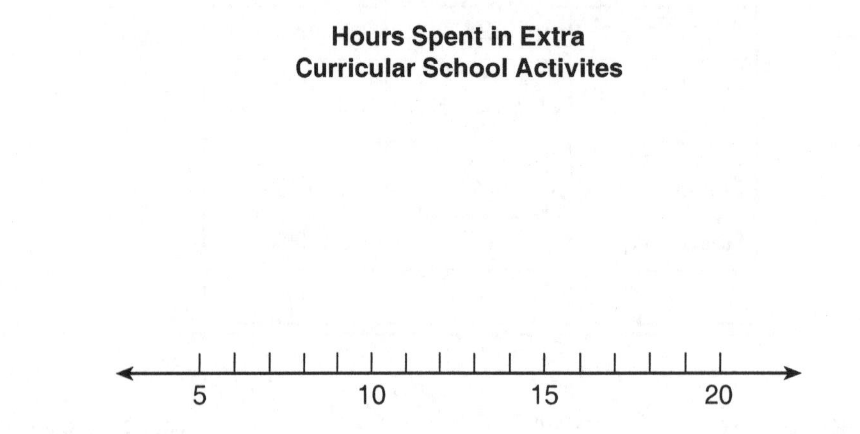

Directions: Use the following line plot to answer Numbers 2 through 4.

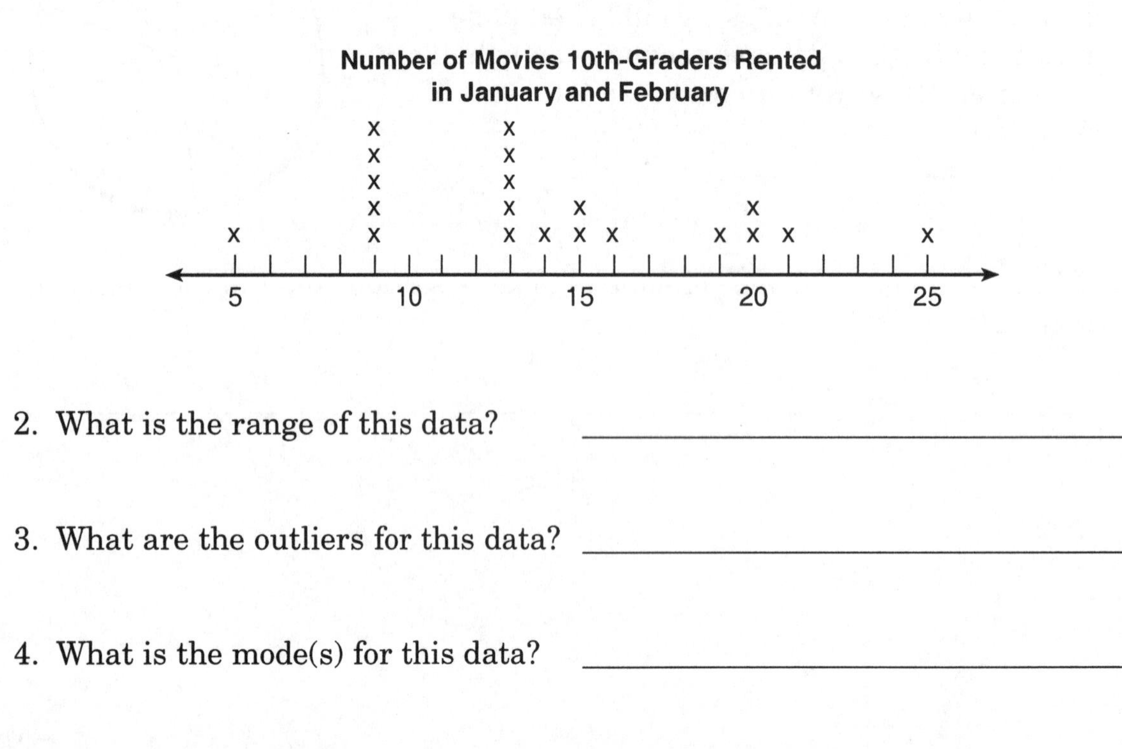

2. What is the range of this data? ____________________

3. What are the outliers for this data? ____________________

4. What is the mode(s) for this data? ____________________

Box plots

A **box plot** (also called a **box-and-whisker plot**) is used when you want to show how a large set of data clusters together. It shows the median, the quartiles, and outliers, but no other specific values. **Quartile** is a word used in statistics to mean one-fourth of the set of data.

Practice

1. The following is a list of the ages (in chronological order) at which the first 21 Presidents of the United States were inaugurated. Make a box-and-whisker plot using this data and the number line below.

   57, 61, 58, 54, 68, 51, 49, 64, 50, 48, 65, 52, 56, 46, 47, 55, 42, 60, 62, 43, 69

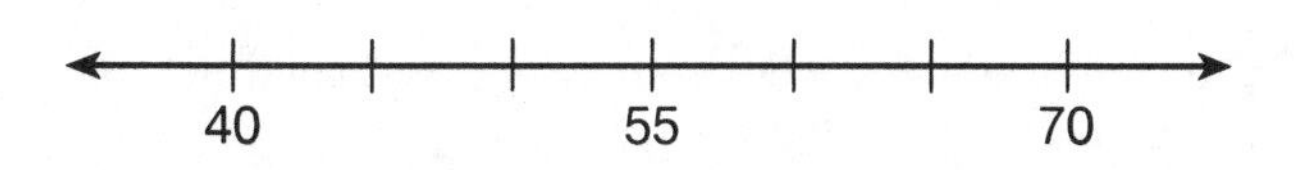

Directions: Use the box-and-whisker plot to answer Numbers 2 through 4.

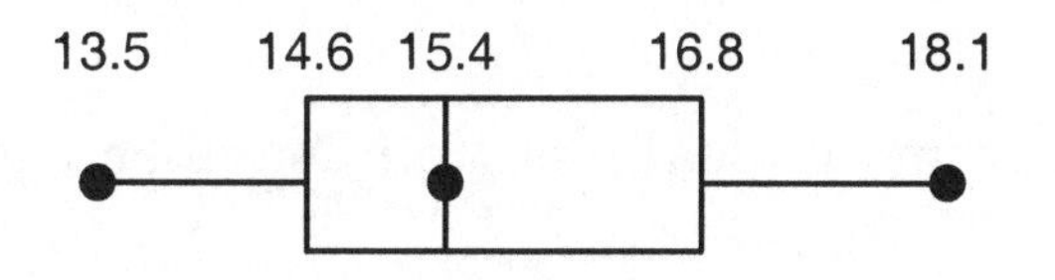

2. What is the median for this set of data? __________

3. What is the lower quartile for this set of data? __________

4. What is the upper extreme for this set of data? __________

Stem-and-leaf plots

A **stem-and-leaf plot** is used when you want to show the shape of the data so that you can quickly identify the greatest, least, and median values in the data.

1. Mrs. McCollum, the 10th-grade physical education instructor, organized pulse rate data for her 1st-period class. The pulse rate was taken after each student had completed one minute of running in place.

   102, 180, 115, 122, 126, 175, 103, 135, 144, 126, 126, 162, 126, 175, 145

   Make a stem-and-leaf plot to summarize this data.

Directions: Use your stem-and-leaf plot from Number 1 to answer the following questions.

2. In what range did the most pulse rates fall? ______________________

3. Were there any holes in the data? If so, identify the empty range.

   ____

4. What was the mode for this data? ______________________

5. What was the median for this data? ______________________

Scatter plots

A **scatter plot** is used when you want to analyze two sets of data and see how closely they are related. You plot corresponding numbers as ordered pairs and decide if they are related by seeing how close they come to forming a straight line.

Practice

1. The table shows the number of hours a student studied for each test and the grade received on the test. Draw a scatter plot to show the data from the table.

Study Time (in hours)	Grade
1.5	80
3	90
1	70
2.5	88
1.5	85
3.5	95
4	98

Correlation

When data comes close to forming a straight, slanted line, there is **strong correlation**. If the line has **positive slope**, there is **positive correlation**. If the line has **negative slope**, there is **negative correlation**. If all the points **do not appear to form a line**, there is **no correlation**.

Directions: Write the type of correlation for each graph in Numbers 1 through 4.

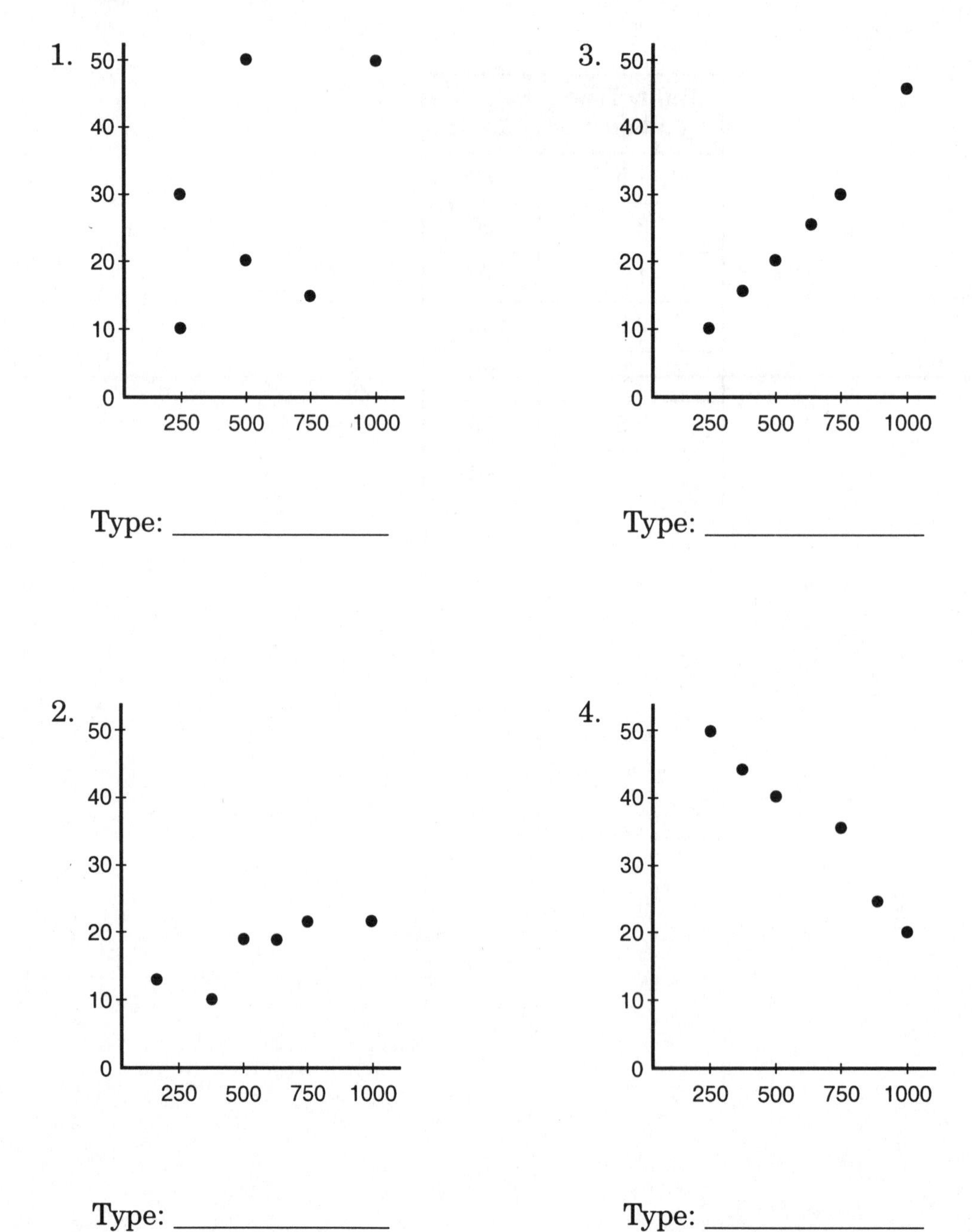

5. The scatter plot below shows the results of a survey of 100 people to see how many would buy "No-Fat Chocolate Malts" at various prices.

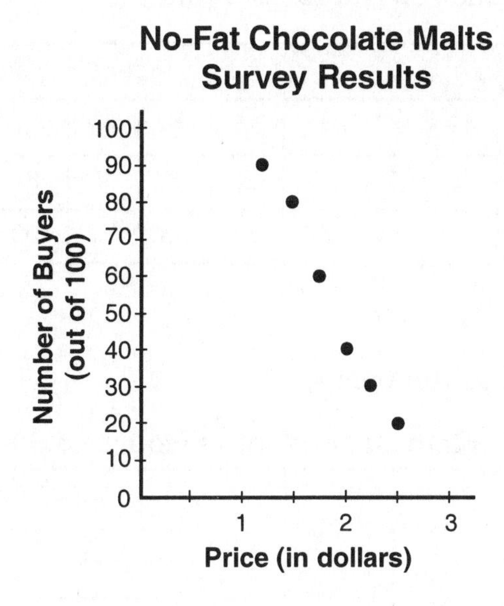

Interpret the data by checking one or more of the following:

______ The two variables are perfectly correlated.

______ The two variables are highly correlated.

______ The two variables are slightly correlated.

______ The two variables are uncorrelated.

______ The two variables are positively correlated.

______ The two variables are negatively correlated.

Directions: The following table shows the number of hours of sleep a group of 10th-grade students got the night before a math test and their math test scores. Use this information to answer Numbers 6 and 7.

	Student											
	#1	#2	#3	#4	#5	#6	#7	#8	#9	#10	#11	#12
Hours of Sleep	9	4	7	6	6	8	9	8	5	7	8	7
Math Test Score	93	71	84	77	82	93	91	100	70	83	90	90

6. Plot the data on the graph below.

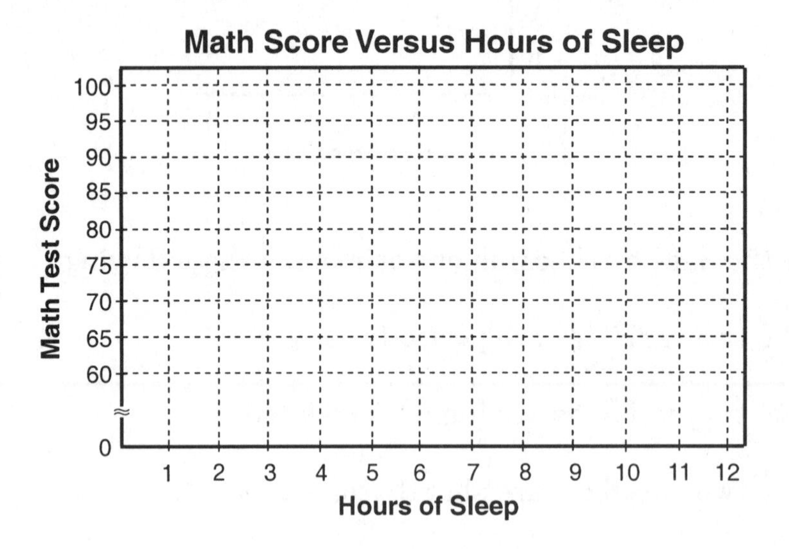

7. Interpret the data by checking one or more of the following:

_______ The two variables are perfectly correlated.

_______ The two variables are highly correlated.

_______ The two variables are slightly correlated.

_______ The two variables are uncorrelated.

_______ The two variables are positively correlated.

_______ The two variables are negatively correlated.

Evaluating Data

The same data can be visually represented in different ways. The table below summarizes which format is usually best for which type of data.

Format	Type of Data
table or chart	organizing numbers
pictograph	comparing amounts
bar graph	comparing amounts
line graph	showing change over time
circle graph	comparing parts of a whole
line plot	showing how data are clustered
box plot	showing how data are clustered
stem-and-leaf plot	showing how data are clustered
scatter plot	showing how data are clustered

Note: When evaluating statistical representations of data, keep the following things in mind:

- Check the **title** and **labels**.
- Study the **scale** and/or **key** used.
- If more than one point in time is represented, identify the overall **trend** of the data.
- If more than one type of data is represented, look for **relationships** between the data points.

? Which format would be best for displaying the results of the survey you created? (page 144)

Practice

Directions: For each situation in Numbers 1 through 5, identify the most appropriate format for the data being collected.

1. You want to know if there is a relationship between students' height and their speed in the 50-yard dash.

   ____

2. You want to show how sales of a new toy have risen and fallen over the last 12 months.

   ____

3. You want to be able to compare the ticket sales of four movies the first month they were shown in theaters.

   ____

4. You want to arrange the names of the frozen yogurt desserts for sale at your store so that customers can see what is offered and how much each one costs.

   ____

5. You want to show how the money earned by the school fund-raiser was divided up to purchase several items for the school.

   ____

The Use and Misuse of Data

Graphs and other data displays can be manipulated so that the same information looks as if it is saying different things.

Example

The table below shows Mr. and Mrs. Vesuvio's income from their pie shop over a period of 8 years.

The Vesuvios' Annual Income over 8 Years

Year	Amount
1991	$18,000
1992	$20,000
1993	$29,000
1994	$27,000
1995	$26,000
1996	$35,000
1997	$34,000
1998	$42,000

In trying to get a loan to expand their business, Mrs. Vesuvio created two graphs with the same data.

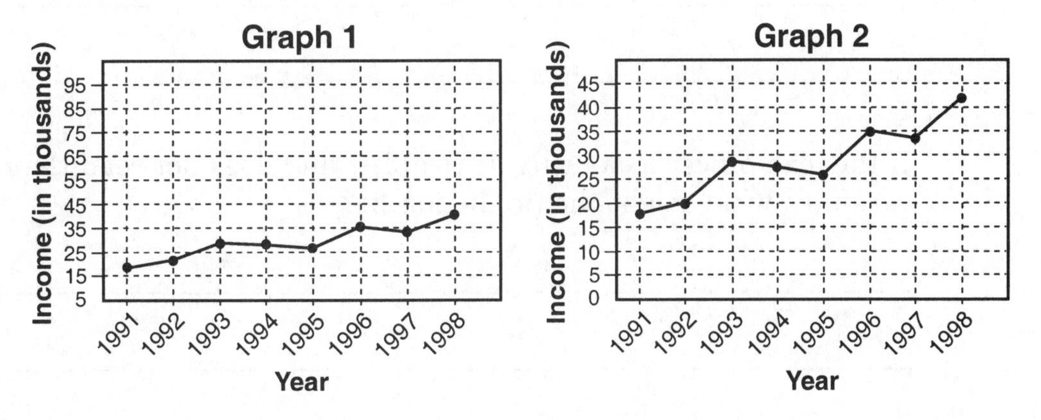

Look carefully at the graphs. Is the data accurate? ______________

Did Mrs. Vesuvio make any mistakes when plotting her points for the line graph?

____

The only difference between the two graphs is the information on the vertical axis.

What are the least and greatest values on the vertical axis in Graph 1?

Least ______________ Greatest ______________

What are the least and greatest values on the vertical axis in Graph 2?

Least ______________ Greatest ______________

What is the scale interval used on Graph 1? ______________

What is the scale interval used on Graph 2? ______________

By changing the range of values and the interval between values on the vertical axis, Mrs. Vesuvio has appeared to change the data, although she has not. One graph makes the data look like it represents a slow, steady increase in income, while the other graph makes the data appear to represent a more dramatic increase.

If the bank's loan officer looks only at Graph 1 and does not read the numbers carefully, what interpretation could that person make?

____

____

____

If the loan officer looks only at Graph 2 and does not read the numbers carefully, what might the prediction be?

____

____

____

Practice

Directions: Use the information below to create two different kinds of graphs. You may use all or part of the information. Remember to title your graphs and label all their parts.

Attendance at Cortazar High School Home Sporting Events

	Boys' Sports		Girls' Sports			
Week # of Season	**Football**	**Basketball**	**Basketball**	**Baseball**	**Track**	**TOTAL**
1	9,200	3,500	2,200	750	200	15,850
2	8,120	2,800	2,005	670	210	13,805
3	6,800	2,900	2,080	700	175	12,655
4	6,200	2,640	2,110	635	200	11,785
5	5,400	2,500	2,350	700	190	11,140
6	3,900	2,450	2,500	740	180	9,770
TOTAL	39,620	16,790	13,245	4,195	1,155	75,005

Making Predictions

When making predictions in mathematical situations, you must be able to spot a trend or pattern and then decide whether to extend the pattern to make a prediction.

1. The following sign was near a rack of T-shirts in a clothing store.

BUY 1 T-shirt	pay $14.99	
BUY 2 T-shirts	pay $26.98 Save $3	off the regular price
BUY 3 T-shirts	pay $38.97 Save $6	
BUY 4 T-shirts	pay $50.96 Save $9	
BUY 5 T-shirts		

Can you predict what the rest of the sign should probably say? ______

Explain. ______________________________

____

____

2. The following table compares pizza prices at five restaurants.

12" Pizza Prices				
Restaurant A	Restaurant B	Restaurant C	Restaurant D	Restaurant E
$7.99	$8.99	$9.50	$8.99	

Can you predict what Restaurant E's price is? ______________

Explain. ______________________________

____

____

3. A wholesale boot company promises delivery of orders of a special line of handmade boots according to the schedule below.

Size of Order	Delivery Time
5 pairs or fewer	4 weeks or less
6–10 pairs	6 weeks or less
11–15 pairs	8 weeks or less

Is it reasonable to make a prediction about what delivery time the company would most likely promise for an order of 24 pairs of handmade boots?

If so, make your prediction. If not, tell why it is not reasonable.

4. Kurt made the following scores on math tests so far this semester: 76, 82, 88. Is it reasonable to make a prediction about his score on the fourth test? If so, make your prediction. If not, tell why it is not reasonable.

Lesson 11: Probability

Probability is a measure of the likelihood that an event will occur.

A **probability of 0** means that the event will not happen. A **probability of 1** means that the event will happen.

For example, what is the likelihood that the sun will come up tomorrow morning? The probability is one. This is an event that will definitely happen. What is the probability that you'll find a real one-thousand dollar bill in the appendix of this workbook? Zero. This is an event that will not happen.

1. A record store will sell 100 raffle tickets for the chance to win any three CDs in the store. Sandra didn't buy any. What is the probability that Sandra will win?

   ____

2. Sandra's friend James decided to buy all 100 raffle tickets. What is the probability that he will win?

   ____

Probability of Simple Events

A **simple event** is an event in which each possible outcome is equally likely to occur. In a coin toss, for example, each of the two possible outcomes, heads and tails, is equally likely. To find the probability of simple events, use the following ratio.

$$P = \frac{\text{number of successful outcomes}}{\text{number of possible outcomes}}$$

1. James decides to give Sandra 8 tickets. Now what is the probability that she will win the CDs?

   ____

2. Now what is the probability that James will win? _______________

3. In another contest, there are six different numbers (1–6) written on pieces of paper and put into a box. To win, you must draw a 5. What is the probability of winning?

   ____

Experimental Probability

Experimental probability is the probability of an event based on an actual experiment.

$$\text{Exp } P\text{ (E)} = \frac{\text{number of actual outcomes of the event}}{\text{number of trials in the experiment}}$$

Practice

The table below shows the outcomes from an experiment in which two coins were tossed ten times. Use this table to answer Numbers 1 through 4.

Tosses	1	2	3	4	5	6	7	8	9	10
Outcomes	HT	HH	TT	TH	HT	TH	TH	HT	HT	TH

H = head T = tail

1. Find Exp *P* (HH). __________

2. Find Exp *P* (TT). __________

3. Find Exp *P* (TH). __________

4. Find Exp *P* (HT). __________

Theoretical probability is used to infer, predict, or guess what will happen. The greater the number of trials in an experiment, the closer the experimental probability will be to the theoretical probability.

Counting Techniques

The **Fundamental Counting Principle (F.C.P.)** is used to find the total number of possible outcomes when a task consists of several separate parts.

1. At Adams High, there are 3 days that a student must take gym. There are 2 sessions offered, and 2 places where the classes meet. Your task is to create a gym class. How many different outcomes are there for this task?

2. The task: Create a password for your e-mail account.

   Restrictions: 4 digits only, first digit 0, repetitions allowed

   Total outcomes: ______________

3. The task: Choose what to eat at a restaurant.

   Restrictions: you must choose one in each category—7 entries, 6 side dishes, 8 desserts, 5 beverages

   Total outcomes: ______________

4. Most radio stations west of the Mississippi River that have four call letters all begin with the letter K. How many different four-letter radio stations are there of this kind?

   ____

Combinations and Permutations

Combination methods apply to **counting subsets**, where repetition of items is not allowed. **Permutation** methods apply to **counting arrangements**, where repetition of items is not allowed.

1. Coach Painter of the Thunderbirds girls' softball team must choose three girls to be starting outfielders from a group of five girls. How many different choices does Coach Painter have to fill these positions?

2. Six students are running a 400-meter race. There will be three medals awarded. How many different outcomes could there be? ____________

3. In how many ways can seven people be seated in a row? ____________

4. To make an ice cream sundae, you get two choices of ice cream from a selection of five flavors. How many different combinations are possible? ____________

In a combination, the order of the choices doesn't affect the final outcome. For example, {A, B} is the same as {B, A}. In a permutation, the order of the choices does affect the final outcome. For example, (A, B) is not the same as (B, A). (**Ordered** pairs—get it?)

Probability of Independent and Dependent Events

Events that have **no influence** on each other are said to be **independent**. Events that **are influenced** by other events are said to be **dependent**.

1. Look at the information in Number 1 on page 164. Draw a tree diagram that shows the outcomes for a gym class based on this information:

   Days: Monday, Wednesday, Friday

   Sessions: A.M. and P.M.

   Places: Gym 1, Gym 2

2. What is the probability that a student will have class on Monday morning in Gym 2?

   ____

To simplify the process of finding probability, multiply the probabilities P_1 and P_2.

For example, in Number 2, you could use the following:

$$P_1 = \frac{1}{3}; \quad P_2 = \frac{1}{2}; \quad P_3 = \frac{1}{2}$$

$$P_1 \bullet P_2 \bullet P_3 = \frac{1}{12}$$

This formula is valuable when constructing a tree diagram would be too time-consuming.

Practice

1. There are 12 marbles in a bag: 4 are red, 4 are black, 3 are green, and 1 is purple. If you reach into the bag and take a marble out, then reach in again and take a second marble without replacing the first, what is the probability of choosing a red marble first, and a green marble second?

____

2. What is the probability of taking a black marble first and a purple marble second (without replacement)?

____

3. There are five questions on a true-or-false quiz. What is the probability that you will get them all right?

____

Probability Based on a Sample

Sometimes you need to collect some data to get an estimate of the probability of an event.

Practice

1. Forty students at Central High School were asked which professional basketball team was their favorite. The table below shows the results.

Team	Number of Students
Chicago Bulls	2
New York Knicks	10
Boston Celtics	24
No favorite	4
TOTAL	40

What is the probability that the next student asked will choose the Boston Celtics?

____

Directions: Use the information given in the previous table to answer Numbers 2 through 4.

2. What is the probability that the next student asked will have **no** favorite team?

____

3. What is the probability that the next student asked will choose the Chicago Bulls?

____

4. Based on the results shown in the table, how many students in a sample of 500 will probably choose the Boston Celtics as their favorite basketball team?

____

Test Your Skills

Directions: The following table shows how far 30 10th-grade students live from school. Use the table to answer Numbers 1 through 3.

Distance from Home to School

	Distance in Miles	Number of Students
	0.5	4
	1	5
	1.5	6
	2	5
	2.5	3
	3	3
	3.5	2
	4	2
TOTAL	18	30

1. What is the mean of the distance traveled to school? (Round to the nearest whole number.)
   A. 1
   B. 2
   C. 3
   D. 4

2. The distance most frequently reported is 1.5 miles. What does this number represent?
   A. the mode
   B. the median
   C. the mean
   D. the frequency

3. How many students travel three or more miles?
   A. 3
   B. 4
   C. 7
   D. 30

4. Below is part of a sand and gravel company's mileage chart showing delivery charges.

Distance from Sellic Sand & Gravel	Delivery Charge
1–12 miles	$19.95
13–18 miles	$27.45
19–24 miles	$34.95
25–30 miles	

Which would be the most likely charge for delivering a load of gravel to a location 36 miles away?

A. $40.45

B. $42.45

C. $49.95

D. $56.95

5. Chad is building a pyramid-shaped display of soup cans at the grocery store where he works. The bottom layer has 7 rows with 7 cans in each row. The second layer has 6 rows with 6 cans in each row. Each succeeding layer has one fewer row with one fewer can in each row. Predict how many cans Chad will need altogether for the display.

A. 140

B. 167

C. 196

D. 259

6. Ed and Alicia go to a snack bar at the beach. The snack bar sells the following items.

Sandwiches	hamburgers	cheeseburgers	hot dogs
Drinks	cola	orange soda	grapefruit juice
Side Orders	french fries	cole slaw	

Alicia says she wants a sandwich, a side order, and a drink. Ed wants to impress her by guessing what she will order. What is the probability that he will guess correctly?

A. $\frac{1}{6}$

B. $\frac{1}{18}$

C. $\frac{3}{8}$

D. $\frac{1}{24}$

7. Gina is fourth in line in the school cafeteria. She sees 8 pieces of pie on the shelf up ahead—3 pieces of key lime pie, 1 piece of pecan pie, and 4 pieces of apple pie. She loves pecan pie, but each of the people in front of her gets to choose before she does. What is the probability that she will get the piece of pecan pie?

____

8. Kyung wins the door prize at a party. He gets to reach into a bag with 9 compact discs in it and take out one of the discs. If he doesn't get the CD he wants on the first try, he is allowed to give away the one he picked and try again. In the bag are 2 hip-hop CDs, 3 pop CDs, 2 rock CDs, and 2 classical CDs. Kyung likes hip-hop and classical music, but he does not like rock or pop. What is the probability that he will pick a CD he does not like on the first try and one that he likes on the second try?

   A. $\frac{1}{24}$

   B. $\frac{2}{9}$

   C. $\frac{25}{72}$

   D. $\frac{5}{18}$

9. Jamal, Mary Ann, and Juanita are the finalists in a competition for the local TV station's annual student recognition award. First prize is $100 and second prize is $50. Jamal and Mary Ann are twins. They are both hoping that one of them will win first prize and the other will win second. It does not matter to them which one wins which prize.

   A. What is the probability that Jamal and Mary Ann, in either order, will take first and second place?

   ____

   B. After school, Jamal and Mary Ann want to go shopping to buy jeans with the prize money. The jeans are on sale for $22 per pair. (Their mother will pay the sales tax.) What is the probability the twins will win enough prize money at the competition to buy each of them a pair of jeans? Explain what this probability means.

   ____

   ____

   ____

10. Which of the following graphs shows growth in sales for Too-Cool Jeans Company?

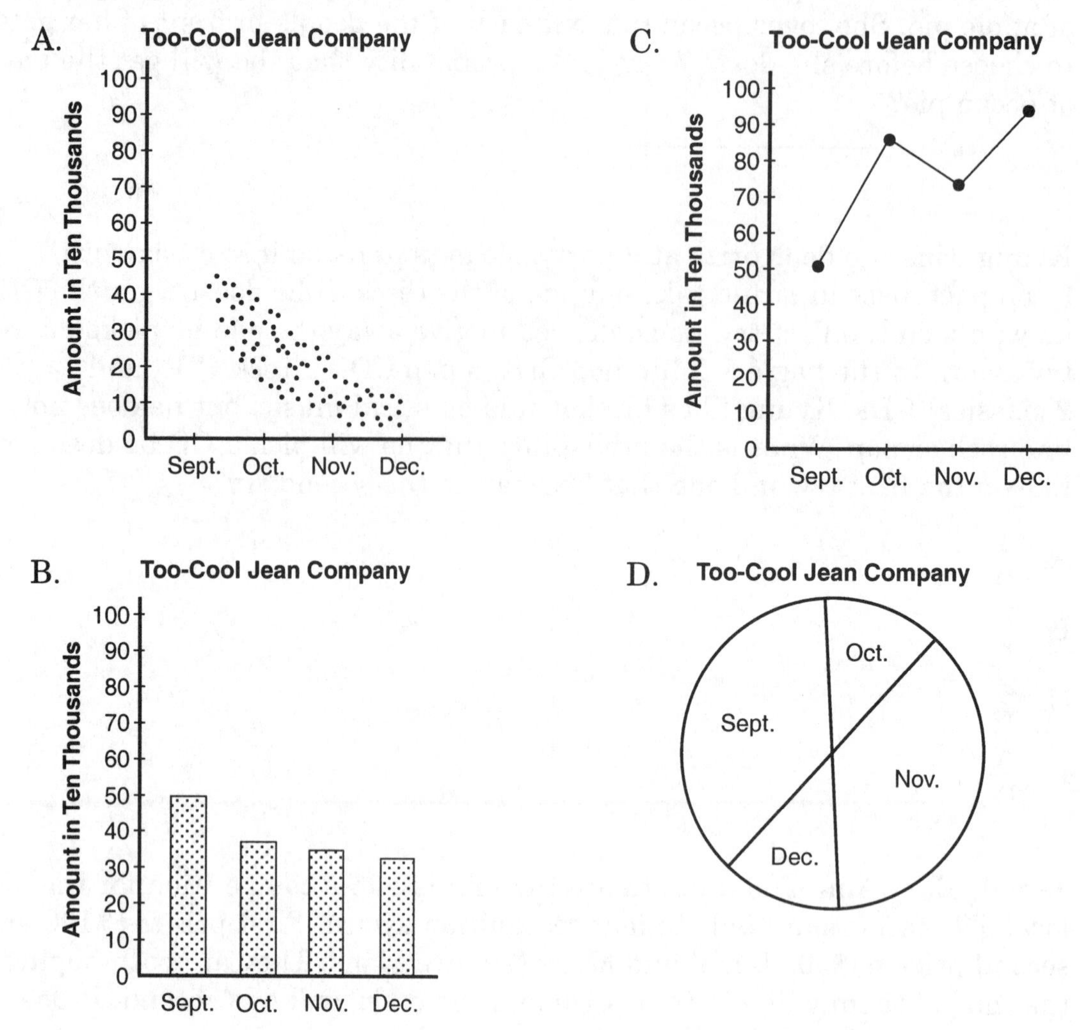

11. Find the median of the following set of test scores.____________

78, 71, 94, 86, 71, 81

12. Find the range of the following set of test scores.____________

98, 78, 71, 62, 94, 86, 71, 81

13. Jeremy and Marian want to know, on the average, how many hours per week students in their geometry class spend doing homework. There are 35 students in the classroom.

    Jeremy decided to ask 10 of his friends in the classroom. Marian decided to stand at the front door of the classroom at the beginning of the class period and ask every third student that enters the classroom.

    Whose set of data, Jeremy's or Marian's, more accurately represents the average hours per week students in their geometry class spend doing homework?

    Explain your answer.______________________________

    ____

    ____

    ____

    ____

14. A survey of 85 students was taken to determine whom they would vote for in the next statewide student government election. Thirty-one said they would vote for Ernster. Based on this sample, about how many votes can Ernster expect if a total of 1,500 students vote in the statewide student government election?

    A. 310
    B. 470
    C. 550
    D. 850

15. Which continent shown in the table has the second smallest range between its highest and lowest points?

World Elevations

Continent	Highest Point	Feet Above Sea Level	Lowest Point	Feet Below Sea Level
Africa	Mt. Kilimanjaro	19,340	Lake Assai	512
Asia	Mt. Everest	29,028	Dead Sea	1,312
Australia	Mt. Kosciusko	7,310	Lake Eyre	52
Europe	Mt. El'brus	18,510	Caspian Sea	92
North America	Mt. McKinley	20,320	Death Valley	282
South America	Mt. Aconcagua	22,834	Valdes Peninsula	131

(lowest point in Antarctica is unknown, so Antarctica is not listed here; source: *World Almanac*)

A. Europe
B. Australia
C. South America
D. North America

Directions: Use the graph to answer Number 16.

16. If the overall trend of this data continues, how many pairs of skis should Sam plan to rent in 1999?

A. 34 pairs
B. 48 pairs
C. 50 pairs
D. 56 pairs

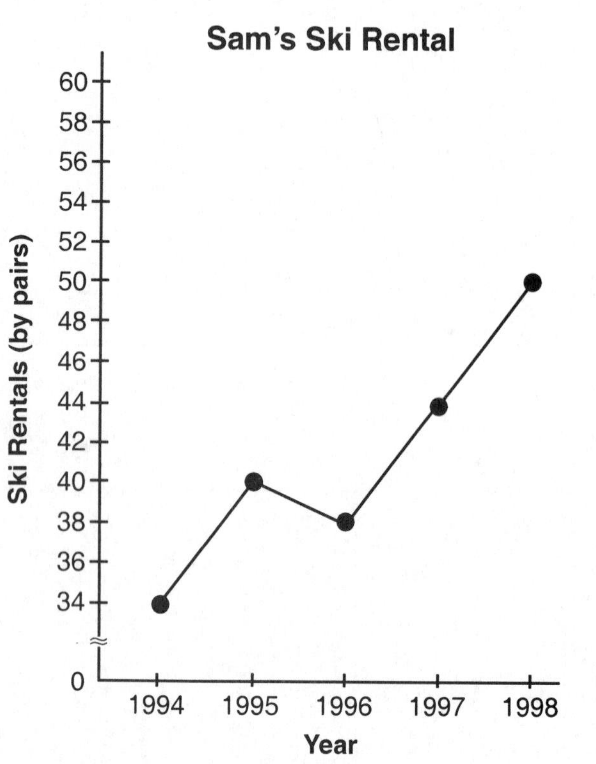

17. The Coffee Shop charges $4.50 per pound of coffee. Delivery charge is $2.00 per order. Which graph represents this data?

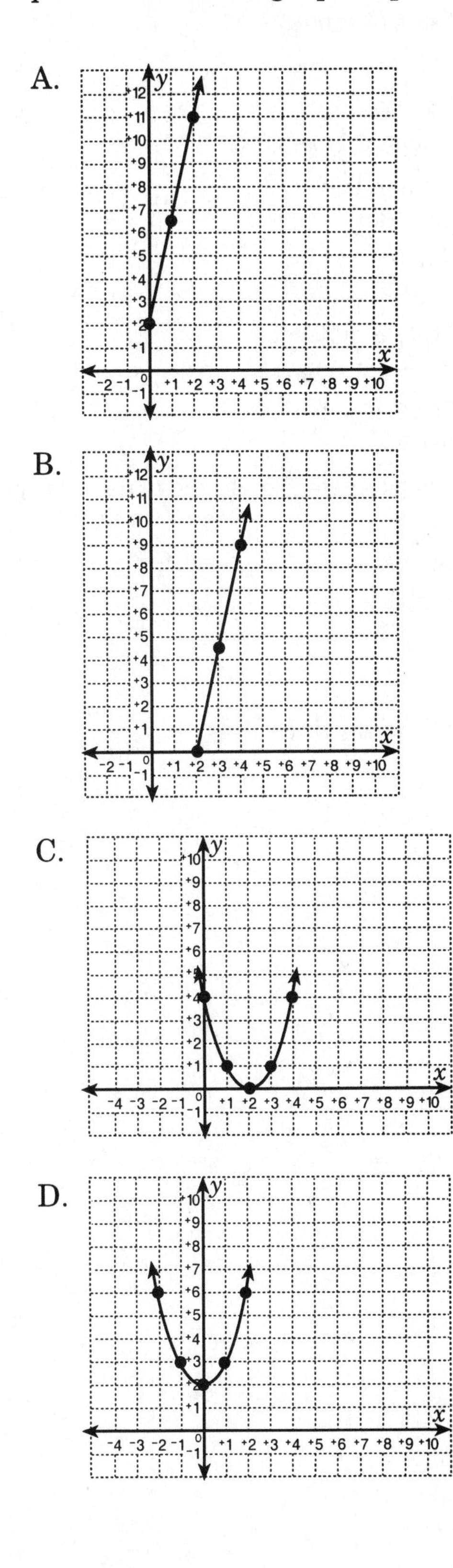

Directions: Use the stem-and-leaf plot to answer Number 18.

18. Which animal has a resting pulse rate of 126?
    A. shark
    B. collie
    C. kangaroo
    D. Boston terrier

Animal Pulse Rates (Resting)

Stem	Leaf	Animal
1	2 6	Whale
2	9	Camel
3	0 5 5	Elephant, Horse, Trout
4	0 2	Donkey, Lion
5	5 5	Cow, Bear
6	6	Giraffe
7	0	Deer
8	0 0	Goat, Groundhog
9	2 5	Pointer, Fox terrier
10	2 6	Collie, Irish terrier
11	6	Dolphin
12	0 0 6 8	Kangaroo, Beagle, Boston terrier, Pekingese
13	2	Cat
14	0	Beaver
15	5	Rabbit

19. Which stem-and-leaf plot represents the following data?

    39, 25, 41, 39, 23, 43, 39, 42, 24, 33

A. **School A**

Stem	Leaf
2	1 1 1
3	1 1 1 1
4	1 1 1

B. **School B**

Stem	Leaf
2	3 4 5
3	3 9 9 9
4	1 2 3

C. **School C**

Stem	Leaf
2	3
3	4
4	5

D. **School D**

Stem	Leaf
2	23 24 25
3	33 39 39 39
4	41 42 43

20. The table to the right shows the scores on a history (H) test and the weight in pounds of 19 high school students.

The highest possible score is 20.

Scores (H)	Weight
20	120
20	165
19	101
18	121
18	150
18	124
17	140
17	133
16	145
16	125
16	110
15	122
15	115
14	180
14	113
14	100
13	134
11	135
9	131

A. Plot the data on the graph below.

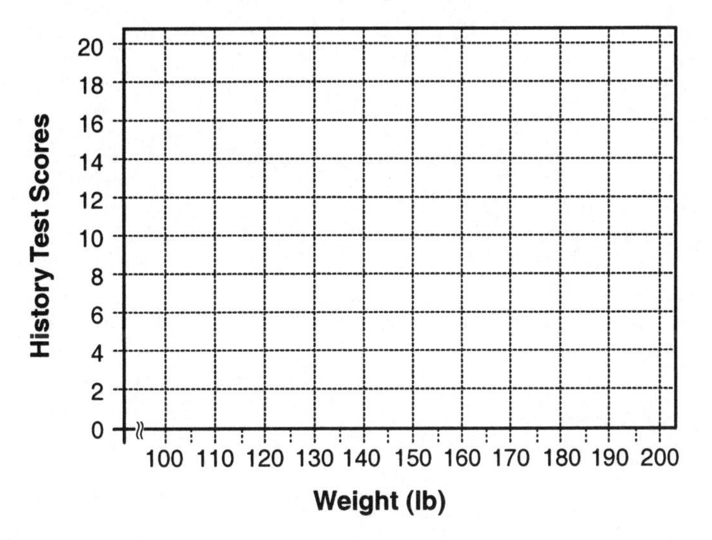

B. What conclusion could you make based on the data?

____

____

____

____

C. Imagine another factor that might have affected the history test scores, such as the number of hours studied or the number of hours slept the night before. Create a list of data for these factors and plot the data on the graph to show how it is related to the history test scores. Explain the relationship on the lines below.

____

____

____

____

APPENDIX A

General Tips for Taking Math Tests

General Tips for Taking Math Tests

The only guaranteed way to pass any math test is to learn the math. If you learn everything in this book, you should ace the state test. Here are a few general tips to keep in mind on test day.

TIP 1: Take your time.

The strategies that follow will require that you spend some extra time as you're taking the test. This will be time well spent. If you practice these strategies in advance and apply the strategies when you take the test, you'll have a much better chance of passing.

TIP 2: Make two passes through the test.

If everybody in your class went through the test and circled the ten hardest problems, each person would pick a different set. What this means is that, for you personally, the hard problems will be mixed in with the easy problems. You need to pay attention to this difficulty issue. Our advice is to make two passes through the test.

On the first pass, skip every problem that seems hard to you. Go all the way from the first question to the last question, working only the easy problems. You might skip ten questions or you might skip thirty questions. The important thing is to solve all of the easy problems before you get frustrated by the hard problems. As you do this, stop and check your work on every problem. Don't think you have the correct answer just because it's one of the choices. Stop and check your work. Then continue to the next question.

On the second pass, solve the harder problems. Remember, you have plenty of time—use it. Try one way and then another to solve each problem.

TIP 3: DO NOT leave any blanks on your answer sheet.

No matter how tired you are at the end of the test, go back and check to make sure you answered every question. If you do not know the answer, then narrow down your choices as much as possible and guess.

TIP 4: Remember to take a step-by-step approach to story and application problems.

In the workbook, you learned how to solve word problems by taking things one step at a time. Here's a quick review of those steps.

Make sure you understand the question. Try to see the operation that is taking place, so that you can pull the math from the problem. Reread the problem to make sure your math works. Do the math. Then, as always, check your work.

TIP 5: Learn to work backward.

What if you can't figure out what to do? There may be a few multiple-choice problems that you can't seem to solve. With practice, you can find instances where it's possible to "plug in" the answer choices and work the problems backward.

Example

To earn a grade of B in science, Nancy needs to score an average of 80 on three tests. On the first test, she scored 85. On the second test, she scored 70. To earn a B, what score does Nancy need on the third test?

A. 70
B. 75
C. 80
D. 85

First, underline the question part of the problem, "what score does Nancy need on the third test?" To work backwards, take one of the choices and try it. If B is the correct answer, Nancy's scores would be 85, 70, and 75. What is the average of these three scores?

____

Since choice B is not big enough, you can cross it out. You can also cross out choice A, because that's even smaller. The correct answer has to be either C or D. If C is the answer, Nancy's scores would be 85, 70, and 80. What is the average of these three scores?

____

If you plug in D, Nancy's scores would be 85, 70, and 85. What is the average of these three scores?

____

TIP 6: Cross out careless choices before you guess.

Sometimes you can't even plug in the choices. Before you guess, check the answers carefully and cross out careless choices.

Example

Martha bought a radio on sale at a 15% discount. If the retail price is normally $60.00, how much did Martha pay for the radio?

A. $ 4.00
B. $ 9.00
C. $45.00
D. $51.00

Look at choice A. If a radio is normally $60.00, do you think Martha is going to get it for only $4.00? Of course not. Cross out A. How about B? Not. Cross it out. Now guess between C and D. If you do this on ten problems, you'll guess about five of them correctly.

TIP 7: On test day, relax.

If you've practiced the material in *Buckle Down on Massachusetts Mathematics, Book 10*, your math skills will be "built-in" by test day. You won't be worried because you'll know that you're prepared. You can relax, knowing that you're ready to do your best.

APPENDIX B

Massachusetts Curriculum Framework: Mathematics Learning Standards, Grade 10

Massachusetts Curriculum Framework: Mathematics Learning Standards, Grade 10

Buckle Down on Massachusetts Mathematics, Book 10, is based on the Massachusetts Mathematics Curriculum Framework Learning Standards for Grades K–10. The workbook has been designed to provide instruction and practice in the skills tested by the Massachusetts Comprehensive Assessment System (MCAS) at Grade 10. The following table matches the learning standards with the *Buckle Down* lessons in which they are addressed.

Learning Standards	*Buckle Down* Units/Lessons
Number Sense	Unit 1
Discrete Mathematics	
• represent problem situations, using discrete structures such as finite graphs, matrices, sequences, and recurrence relations	Lessons 2, 3, & 11
• represent and analyze finite graphs, using matrices	
Mathematical Structure	
• compare and contrast the real number system and its subsystems with regard to structural characteristics	Lesson 1
• demonstrate the logic of algebraic procedures and their interrelationships with geometric ideas and concepts	
Estimation	
• use estimation strategies to judge the reasonableness of results of computation and problem solving involving real numbers	Lessons 2 & 10
• use estimation when making graphs	
Patterns, Relations, and Functions	Unit 2
Algebra	
• formulate problems that involve variable quantities with expressions, equations, and inequalities	Lesson 4
• simplify algebraic expressions to solve equations and inequalities	
Functions	
• model real-world phenomena with a variety of functions	Lessons 5 & 10
• represent and analyze relationships, using tables, verbal rules, equations, and graphs	
• translate among tabular, symbolic, and graphical representations of functions	
Trigonometry	
• apply trigonometry to problem situations involving right triangles	Lesson 6

Learning Standards	*Buckle Down* Units/Lessons
Geometry and Measurement	Unit 3
Geometry and Spatial Sense	
• interpret and draw three-dimensional objects	Lessons 7 & 9
• develop and defend conclusions	
• formulate counter examples	
• construct proofs for mathematical assertions, including indirect proofs and proofs by mathematical induction	
Measurement	
• represent problem situations with geometric models and apply properties of figures	Lessons 7, 8, & 9
• classify figures in terms of congruence and similarity and apply these relationships	
• deduce properties of, and relationships between, figures from given assumptions	
Geometry from an Algebraic Perspective	
• translate between synthetic and coordinate representations	Lessons 4, 7, 8, & 9
• deduce properties of figures, using transformations and coordinates	
• identify congruent and similar figures, using transformations	
• develop and explain geometric interpretations and applications of slope	
Statistics and Probability	Unit 4
Statistics	
• construct, draw inferences, and reason with charts, tables, and graphs that summarize data from real-world situations	Lessons 3 & 10
• use sampling to recognize and describe its role in statistical claims	
• design a statistical experiment to study a problem, conduct the experiment, and interpret and communicate the outcomes	
Probability	
• use simulations to estimate probabilities	Lesson 11
• determine the likelihood of outcomes, using theoretical probabilities	